ORGANIZING
OUTDOOR
VOLUNTEERS

SECOND EDITION

Also available from the Appalachian Mountain Club

The Conservationworks Book
Lisa Capone

Trail Building and Maintenance
Robert D. Proudman and Reuben Rajala

Backcountry Facilities
Design and Maintenance
R.E. Leonard, E.L. Spencer, and H.J. Plumley

AMC Trail Guides
Guide to Mt. Desert Island and Acadia National Park
Guide to Mt. Washington and the Presidential Range
Hiking the Mountain State (West Virginia)
Maine Mountain Guide
Massachusetts and Rhode Island Trail Guide
North Carolina Hiking Trails
White Mountain Guide

Short Hikes and Ski Trips Around Pinkham Notch
A Day Tripper's Guide to the Mt. Washington Area
Linda Buchanan Allen

AMC River Guides
Maine
Massachusetts/Connecticut/Rhode Island
New Hampshire/Vermont

ORGANIZING OUTDOOR VOLUNTEERS

SECOND EDITION

Roger L. Moore, Vicki LaFarge,
and Charles L. Tracy

APPALACHIAN MOUNTAIN CLUB
BOSTON, MASSACHUSETTS

Cover Photo: Carl Demrow
Book Design: Carol Bast Tyler

Copyright © 1992 by the Appalachian Mountain Club.

Published by Appalachian Mountain Club Books with support from
the Rivers, Trails, and Conservation Assistance Program of the
National Park Service.

Distributed by The Talman Company.

ISBN 1-878239-16-3

Library of Congress Card Number   92-22621

All rights reserved. No part of this work may be reproduced or trans-
mitted in any form or by any means, electronic or mechanical, including photocopy, recording, or any information storage or retrieval
system, without permission in writing from the publisher.

The paper used in this publication meets the minimum requirements
of the American National Standard for Information Sciences—Perma-
nence of Paper for Printed Library Materials, ANSI Z39.48–1984.∞

Printed on recycled paper.   ✪

Printed in the United States of America.

10 9 8 7 6 5 4 3 2 1   92 93 94 95 96 97

Contents

This manual is dedicated to the volunteers and staff of conservation organizations everywhere. They give up weekends, evenings, and holidays to sweat, struggle, laugh, and enjoy a labor of love for the lands, rivers, and conservation causes in which they believe. Without them and the work they do, this planet would become a stark place indeed.
Thank you!

Foreword

THE 1990S IS THE DECADE to take that overused maxim—think globally, act locally—and turn it on its head.

With the heightened environmental awareness of the last several years, it seems that almost every conversation touches on toxic waste, ozone holes, rain forest destruction, and other problems. Awareness is a step in the right direction, but it often leaves the individual feeling incapable of changing things for the better.

And yet, if you look closer to home—the revitalized urban park, the protected watershed, the burgeoning trail or greenway—you'll see that citizens can and do make positive changes for the environment, right in their own communities. Citizen groups are finding that they are able to take on projects of all sizes by creating effective volunteer organizations. With the proper supports in place (a clear purpose and goal, work plans, financing, and volunteers), these new "conservation corps" are translating their ideas into action. The results are inspiring: cleaner rivers, new recreational corridors, protected landscapes, and renewed wildlife habitat. The success of these ventures does more than simply clean things up; it also builds a stronger sense of community and rekindles our respect for the land.

Today towns, cities, and states across the country are facing financial constraints and increased burdens that are likely to continue through the decade and beyond. Where the government has had to leave off, volunteer groups can fill the void by identifying conservation needs, building local support, and going to work. Municipalities and agencies, though short on funds or personnel to assign to new projects, can often provide guidance and technical advice to such organizations.

Citizen groups have the potential to make vast improvements in our country's landscape by virtue of their commitment and the swiftness with which they can address conservation projects and environmental problems close to home. School groups can join in on projects and, while they are at it, learn the basics of ecology and earth science. Civic groups, churches, recreation groups, and many others are ready and waiting for someone to show them the way.

You are in a position to make things happen. Friends and neighbors will value the chance to help improve their environment, and your children and grandchildren will be the beneficiaries of your hard work. So go ahead: act locally. You can make a difference.

—Andrew J. Falender
Executive Director
Appalachian Mountain Club

Preface

IN 1982, the Appalachian Mountain Club embarked on an adventure called the National Volunteer Project (NVP). Its premise was simple—users of public land should help take care of "their" lands. We found that this could best be accomplished by helping these users organize for coordinated, "hands-on" action in partnership with government land-managing agencies. Six new volunteer organizations were created as a result of the NVP. All are still working and several of them have flourished.

This book presents a step-by-step approach to organizing a group of any size for any duration to meet any conservation need that you determine is important. The approaches and pointers contained here have broad applicability. They have all been tested and proven in the field, with volunteers from the Everglades to the Pacific Northwest having had a hand in their development. We hope you find *Organizing Outdoor Volunteers* helpful as you go about your part in helping to keep our great outdoors great.

There are countless people who have played important roles in making this book possible. While it would be impossible to thank them all, special thanks are in order to some.

First, we would like to recognize the National Park Service (which provided funding for this project) and specifically Steven Golden of the Rivers, Trails, and Conservation

Assistance Program for the North Atlantic Region. Steve cooked up the notion of getting the ideas contained here into the hands of the volunteers who can use them most. We thank him for recognizing the need and giving us the chance to write.

Second, our thanks go to all who contributed to the first edition of this book. That book, which was the final report of the NVP, represented the combined efforts and experience of thousands of dedicated volunteers. All of them deserve credit for much of what is contained here, but there are some we would like to thank especially. The talented volunteers who planned and led the NVP as members of the NVP Steering Committee have earned our deepest thanks. They are Charles Burnham, Jay Coburn, Michael Cohen, Steven Golden, Sally Holland, William Kemsley, Andrea Lukens, Steven Nelmes, Nelson Obus, and Sally Schnitzer—thank-you! For his written contributions to the first edition of this book, we gratefully acknowledge Michael Cohen for the Leadership Development, Motivation, and Team Building sections. Many thanks also to Carol Phipps, whose insights and production assistance never seemed to end.

Special thanks are in order to the Richard King Mellon Foundation, which provided funding for the NVP, and to Tom Deans, former Executive Director of the AMC. It was Tom's vision that pushed us to propose the NVP, and it would have never happened without his continued hard work and support.

And finally, to everyone out there who worked with us and learned with us—thank you most of all.

—The authors

Introduction

About Grassroots Conservation Organizations

THE PURPOSE OF THIS MANUAL is to help you—private citizens, volunteer leaders, government land managers—to find, motivate, and organize other like-minded citizens to conserve and manage natural resources. It is a "how-to" book that presents a practical, step-by-step, hands-on approach to starting and/or strengthening conservation organizations. It will also help you to identify sources for additional help.

Volunteer action is an important premise of this program. We start from the viewpoint that personal, private-citizen involvement in organized conservation groups is effective and necessary. There are many compelling reasons for this:

There Is a Tremendous Amount of Work to Be Done.

The United States has one of the greatest wealths of natural resources of any nation on earth, but these resources are at risk from overuse and unwise use that threaten their preservation.

Government Agencies Cannot Do It All.

Demand for outdoor recreation opportunities and the need for conservation efforts keep increasing while the budgets for most public agencies have decreased in recent years. In addition, government agencies aren't responsible for much of the recreation and conservation land outside the state and national park systems.

Locals Understand Local Needs.

Local residents are likely to understand which natural resources and recreation opportunities are most significant. These residents are in a good position to tap local resources to meet these needs.

Involved Citizens Become More Educated and Credible.

When people actually roll up their sleeves and try to address a need, they begin to understand it better. That understanding and credibility make an active volunteer organization a powerful advocate with their peers and in the political process.

Users Have Knowledge and Skills that Are Essential.

Expert conservation work is not limited just to those with advanced degrees in ecology or environmental sciences. All professions and skills can make contributions.

There Is a Leadership Need in Conservation.

There is always more work to do and government cannot do it all. Local organizing for local projects and private protection of lands not managed by the government are a great part of America's conservation heritage.

Volunteerism Works.

Since the late nineteenth century, the volunteers of the Appalachian Mountain Club have built and maintained public trails in America's Northeast. The 1,200-mile Appalachian Trail was conceived, built, and is now maintained almost entirely by volunteers under the coordination of the Appalachian Trail Conference. The advocacy of John Muir, the Sierra Club, and many others is responsible for preserving a great deal of the land called "public" today. The Nature Conservancy has helped establish a Natural Heritage Program in every state. These and many other examples of citizen involvement have created a tradition of active and *successful* democracy in conservation.

The Role of Grassroots Conservation Organizations

Simply put, a grassroots conservation organization is any group of concerned citizens who come together to actively address a conservation need. Note the most important words in this definition: *together, active, conservation.* Let's look at each one:

Together. Whether associating for a single workday or formally organizing "forever," there are distinct benefits to working together. Organizations provide:

1. *Greater Accomplishment.* Volunteers working together can get more done than individuals acting alone.

2. *Pride of Accomplishment.* The pride of accomplishing more through teamwork can be a motivational engine itself. One success creates the energy for further effort.

3. *Esprit de Corps.* Camaraderie is an important by-product of an effective grassroots organization. It keeps motivation up, even during frustrating or discouraging times.

4. *Fun and Social Interaction.* For most people, working with others is more enjoyable than toiling alone. We continue doing what we enjoy.

Active. Our definition stresses active involvement. Meetings where concerned conservationists talk about the issues, and less active efforts like letter-writing campaigns are important, but organizing people to get outside, roll up their sleeves, and get their hands dirty has some compelling advantages:

Active, constructive involvement is the key to successful conservation work. Here volunteers install a bridge on the March Cataract Trail, Mount Greylock, Massachusetts.

1. *More Fun.* Most of us like mud, sweat, and beers more than stamps, phones, and drones. Yes, the latter are sometimes necessary, but the former can make them a lot more tolerable and accomplish important work in the process.

2. *More Meaningful.* An acre of trees planted has more impact than a discussion about the need to plant trees.

3. I*mmediate Results and Rewards.* Sharing the reward of looking back over a hard day's accomplishments with good friends is a joy and a powerful motivator as well.

4. *Builds Experience and Credibility.* Hands-on experience makes people better planners and advocates. They understand the complexities of the issues better and gain more credibility in the decision-making arena.

Conservation. That's the whole purpose of organizing, and it can take many different forms. Below is a very small sample of some of the activities that grassroots conservation organizations undertake:

1. *Trails* (pedestrian, equestrian, mountain bike, motorized, etc.)
      Planning
      Construction
      Maintenance
      Management

2. *Rivers*
      Corridor Planning
      Protection
      Rehabilitation
      Management

3. *Land Protection and Management*
    Resource Inventories
    Negotiations and Purchase
    Landowner Relations
    Boundary Marking
    Property Monitoring

4. *Conservation*
    Tree Planting
    Policy Making
    Litter/Dump Removal
    Exotic Species Control
    Timber Management

5. *Water Cleanup*
    Preparation of Environmental Compliance
        Documents
    Cleanup

6. *Wildlife Management*
    Controlling Exotic and Feral Species
    Animal Rescue
    Rehabilitation of Injured Animals
    Reintroduction of Native Species
    Protection/Propagation of Rare and
        Endangered Species

7. *Recreation Management*
    Campground Management/Operations
    Facility Repair/Maintenance/Operations
    Hunter Safety Courses
    Construction of Facilities
    User Counts
    Visitor Impact Management
    Management Planning

8. *Research*
>   Wildlife Monitoring
>   Gathering Baseline Data
>   Environmental Quality Monitoring
>   Providing Input to Management Plans
9. *Education/Interpretation*
>   Naturalist Programming
>   User Education/Information
>   Guiding Hikes
>   Historic Preservation
>   Historic Reenactments
>   Public Information

As you can see, there are many tasks to consider. Don't become overwhelmed. There are many ways that an association of concerned citizens could take on a manageable piece of this work. Different grassroots organizations can vary on a number of important dimensions: size, length of commitment, focus, and level of sophistication.

Size. All grassroots organizations start with a small number of concerned people and grow from there. How big these organizations become (or need to become) depends a lot on how they define their goals. Some important tasks can be carried out by organizations with fewer than ten "members" while other activities require hundreds or thousands of people. At one end of the grassroots spectrum are groups of five or six friends who "adopt" their favorite areas. At the other end is the Sierra Club with over 600,000 members.

Length of Commitment. Groups may come together only once or for short periods to accomplish specific projects. Consider the concerned volunteers who mobilize a cleanup after an oil spill. Other groups may feel that their cause warrants a permanent organization. A "friends" of a local park group may span many generations.

Focus. Some groups focus on a single need such as protecting a specific natural area. Others have a broader agenda like "improving the quantity and quality of public lands in Colorado" or "promoting safe and environmentally sound hang gliding throughout the United States." Missions can vary by geography, type and breadth of activity, and approach.

Level of Sophistication. Some groups keep things very simple and achieve excellent results. Others incorporate as nonprofit corporations, employ many complex methods, and enter into sophisticated relationships with other organizations to accomplish their goals.

Volunteer Partnerships

Perhaps the most sophisticated form a grassroots organization can take is that of the "volunteer partnership." This is a group of organized volunteers (often a nonprofit organization) that works in cooperation with a government agency to achieve conservation goals. The volunteer organization takes on significant long-term responsibilities as opposed to short-term tasks.

Volunteer partnerships have three important characteristics:

AMC volunteers repairing trail cairns near Nelson Crag in the White Mountains of New Hampshire—an example of private efforts on public lands.

- There is mutual respect, trust, and regular communication between the organized volunteers and the government agency staff.
- They accept meaningful land management responsibilities. Partners do not simply advise, they get things done.
- The volunteer partner is generally supportive and cooperative, not adversarial.

Volunteer partnerships can offer significant advantages over other types of volunteer programs. Among these advantages are:

Sense of Ownership and Responsibility. Being "officially" responsible for something important has a way of bringing out the best in people and organizations. When a worker's "signature" is on any piece of work, that worker wants it to be the best, whether that worker is one person or a whole group.

Long-term Continuity. The ongoing nature of the volunteer organization provides long-term continuity.

Self-contained Management. Volunteer organizations manage their own recruiting, training, supervision, recognition, and evaluation. This can save agency resources and accomplish more.

Teamwork. This allows for greater accomplishment and reward.

Communication. The volunteer organization provides the agency partner with a single contact (or a few) in their group who communicates with many volunteer workers.

New Blood and Challenge. The partnership infuses the agency with different skills, enthusiasm, and friendly competition. This prompts each partner to accomplish more than either could alone (i.e., the whole is greater than the sum of its parts).

Grassroots conservation organizations come in all shapes and sizes, from the small, informal, focused group of friends to the large, permanent, nonprofit corporation. There is room for both and all the permutations in between. Diversity and flexibility are the great strength of grassroots conservation organizations and make them an important force in conservation.

Case Studies of Successful Volunteer Conservation Organizations

W E HAVE DISCUSSED what grassroots conservation organizations are and why they are important.
Now, let's look at some examples of actual groups that are
thriving on the front lines of grassroots conservation work:

Portland Trails

In 1988, half a dozen like-minded citizens of Portland,
Maine, met at a public review of the Portland Shoreway
Access Plan, a comprehensive study of public access to the
city's shorelines and open space commissioned by the city
council. The Portland Shoreway Access Plan recommendations were formally adopted by the city council, but
more important, they captured the interest of this small
group, which loosely organized itself in 1989 as the Portland Shoreway Access Coalition (PSAC). In its first year,
the coalition pursued one of the Shoreway Access Plan's
most promising recommendations, development of a three-

mile shoreline trail connecting Portland's downtown with the Fore River Sanctuary, a seventy-acre conservation area owned by the Maine Audubon Society. With help from the National Park Service's (NPS) Conservation Assistance Program and the Appalachian Mountain Club, PSAC formulated a land protection strategy for the trail and organized a series of volunteer trail days.

The following year, the group encountered significant obstacles. First, they faced the daunting task of obtaining a complex series of permits for a proposed pedestrian bridge over the Fore River. Second, some of the landowners along the proposed trail refused to allow shoreline access. Nevertheless, the group continued to organize volunteer trail days on selected trail segments. A new planning intern provided much-needed staffing to coordinate activities and to apply for several small grants. At the suggestion of the National Park Service, the group gradually began to take on a broader role for itself, beyond the Fore River Trail. By the end of 1990, the group had determined that there was a need for a citywide trail advocacy group and formed a nonprofit organization: Portland Trails.

In 1991, Portland Trails made the leap from an informal coalition focusing on a single trail to Portland's most visible trails advocate, promoting a network of trails linking the city's parks, marshes, rivers, and shoreline. Hands-on trail work continued through a series of trail days at a neglected city park. The group produced a "vision map" of the Portland Trails network, developed in conjunction with the city's park commission. Portland Trails also worked with other groups at the state and local level to revive interest in securing an abandoned rail corridor, identified as a key trail link by the Portland Shoreway Access Plan.

More challenges faced Portland Trails in 1992 as the group took on a membership drive and institution of an annual program of events. Although many of the problems relating to the establishment of the Fore River Trail remained, the group continued to build its capacity for handling these difficult issues. More important, through their advocacy, trails and public access have become a part of Portland's social and political agenda. In his June 1991 inaugural address, Mayor Thomas Allen identified connecting open space and assuring pubic shoreline access as among his top priorities.

Mystic River/Whitford Brook Watershed Association

Promoting southeastern Connecticut's Mystic River as a shared resource, rather than as the natural boundary separating four communities, has been the unifying theme of this watershed association. In the summer of 1988, a forum organized by the conservation commissions of the four Mystic River towns explored the possibility of an intercommunity river planning initiative. Representatives from the National Park Service's Conservation Assistance Program were also invited to attend the forum and consider participating in the development of a river protection effort. The communities had learned of this unique Park Service program, which assists groups working to protect rivers and establish trails, through the office of their local U.S. representative, Sam Gejdenson.

Following the forum, the four communities decided to make a formal request for NPS assistance. (A formal letter of request is essentially all that is required to apply for the

NPS Conservation Assistance Program. The letter should state clearly the scope of the project and the goals of NPS involvement. Successful applicants like the Mystic River/Whitford Brook group demonstrate solid local support and clear objectives leading to tangible conservation achievements.) Through the subsequent involvement of the National Park Service, a four-town citizen advisory committee was formed early the following year.

Initially, the committee included only two representatives from each community. However, due to high citizen interest, the advisory committee soon numbered thirty volunteers. Through a series of six monthly workshops facilitated by NPS, the committee identified and discussed the resource issues affecting the watershed.

Volunteers constructing a fish ladder along Whitford Brook in southeastern Connecticut.

At the conclusion of the workshops the committee issued an action plan that highlighted critical resource issues and recommended short- and long-term actions. Foremost among the immediate actions was the establishment of a permanent river organization. The action plan also called for two immediate short-term "hands-on" projects.

The first hands-on project was installation of a small fish ladder to expand the habitat for anadromous fish. As it happened, the location of the proposed fish ladder straddled the boundary of three of the four watershed communities and thus served to further cooperation. The three towns each agreed to contribute either funding or in-kind labor to support the fish ladder, and a local chapter of Trout Unlimited rounded out the needed funding.

With technical assistance from the River Watch Network, the group also began a volunteer water quality monitoring program. This project was another tangible response to the primary issue facing the river. Both of these projects helped to maintain a practical focus on improving the river environment during the early stages of the organization's development.

By the spring of 1990, the Mystic River/Whitford Brook Watershed Association had established itself as a formal nonprofit organization. Six months later the fish ladder was in place. Within a year, the group was distributing a newsletter with the results of its second round of water monitoring. Currently, the Watershed Association is working to increase its membership and broaden the involvement of local schools in the water quality monitoring program.

Organizers walking the Bay Circuit Trail in Ipswich, Massachusetts.

The Bay Circuit Alliance

The idea of a "Bay Circuit" in eastern Massachusetts was originally introduced in 1929. It was to be a greenway corridor of open spaces and parks that would form a 120-mile arc of protected lands through fifty communities in the suburbs around Boston. The north and south end points of the Bay Circuit were on the shores of Massachusetts Bay—hence the name. Unfortunately, the original plans were never put into effect.

In November 1989 the Massachusetts Department of Environmental Management (DEM) convened a meeting of conservation and recreation groups interested in the Bay Circuit. They discussed organizing a private coalition that would work in partnership with DEM's Bay Circuit Program to establish a Bay Circuit Trail—a recreational path that would connect protected lands within the circuit. However, amid questions about the feasibility of the trail and the need for yet another conservation organization, reception for the proposal was lukewarm.

Another idea sparked interest, though: an exploratory trek of the potential routes for the Bay Circuit Trail. Groups such as the Massachusetts Audubon Society, the Appalachian Mountain Club, and the National Park Service were enthusiastic. In June 1990, the first Bay Circuit Trek took place. For seven days, participants combined hiking, biking, and paddling the entire Bay Circuit corridor.

In three ways, the trek turned a private, volunteer conservation coalition into an ongoing Bay Circuit advocacy group. First, the trek convinced the core group of trail proponents that a trail was feasible. Second, the trek's planning and execution identified the local groups and individuals with a genuine interest in planning and developing the trail—the "constituency" of the new group. Finally (and perhaps most important from the standpoint of attracting volunteers), the media coverage emphasized the fun the participants had.

After the trek, planning for the Bay Circuit Trail commenced at the local level and in the fall of 1990, the first segment of the Bay Circuit Trail was officially dedicated. Similarities in the kinds of issues faced by local Bay Circuit Trail planning committees began to give more substance to the need for a coordinating advocacy group—the Bay Circuit Alliance.

A year after the first meeting, the niche for the Bay Circuit Alliance continued to take shape. An informal steering committee began to explore the feasibility of starting a nonprofit organization and sponsored Trek II. The second trek built on the successes of the previous year. Local groups and individuals got involved, and changes in the actual routing highlighted the last year's advances in local trail planning and development.

After Trek II the steering committee applied for and secured two grants to formally organize the Bay Circuit Alliance as a nonprofit organization and to support distribution of a newsletter and other trail-planning activities. Another series of volunteer trail days culminated in the official opening of a second segment of the Bay Circuit Trail in the fall of 1991. Next steps for the Bay Circuit Alliance include building a membership base of organizations and individuals and strengthening its ability to work in partnership with DEM and other state agencies.

Observations

Even though the organizations described above are quite different, notice that they share five common characteristics that enabled them to get off to fast starts and to sustain high levels of effectiveness. Each successful group:

Has a Clear, Compelling Vision. The organization has a vision of the way things should be in its area of concern and a concrete plan for how it will make that vision a reality.

Provides a Constructive and Rewarding Outlet. From its beginning the group organizes and carries out action-oriented, hands-on work projects that are rewarding and constructive.

Makes Regular Progress. The group's activities get it closer to the realization of its vision. It is not just spinning its wheels.

Attracts New People. Successful groups and causes are contagious. They are able to recruit new volunteers and supporters continuously.

Is Fun. The work of these groups is not a grind. New volunteers are not becoming more and more creative in their excuses not to attend a second project. These groups and the people involved in them are fun!

When all is said and done, what determines whether a grassroots conservation organization is a success? A successful organization performs well in all the five areas noted above. Reword them as questions and use them as "measures of success" for your organization. Design your group with them in mind and evaluate its performance regularly on each of these measures.

So far we've seen the why and what of grassroots conservation organizations. Now let's move on to how to organize a conservation group.

Phase One

Startup and Recruitment

L ET'S SAY YOU SEE A NEED to create a local conservation organization or to strengthen an existing one. Where do you begin? While there is no magic formula for getting off the ground, successful efforts usually include these components: identifying a mission that addresses a real conservation need; cultivating support in the community by persuading others of this need; creating a core group of people committed to your cause; cultivating financial support; and sponsoring meaningful and enjoyable activities that help you accomplish your mission.

Assess the Needs and Identify the Mission

Grassroots conservation organizations that don't have a clear and compelling mission rarely last long. Creating such a mission depends on identifying a real conservation need, and meeting this need provides a purpose and focus for the organization and its members. If no clear need exists, it is difficult to find projects on a continuing basis that volunteers will find meaningful. High-caliber volunteers will immediately sense that their efforts are going to make-work activities and quickly find more useful things to do. The absence of a clear need also reduces the coopera-

Getting started means having a plan, the right tools, and enthusiastic volunteers—of any age.

tion you will get from other conservation organizations, government agencies, the press, and sources of funding.

In assessing the need for your organization and in identifying its mission, it is important to ask the following questions:

- Are there unmet conservation needs in the area that could realistically be served by a grassroots conservation organization?

- What conservation needs are now being met and by whom?

- Who are the principal players in area conservation efforts on both the government and volunteer levels? How supportive are they likely to be?

- Is someone else already doing it? Does it make more sense to create a new group or to support the efforts of an existing volunteer group?

Don't depend just on your own "gut sense" for the answers to these questions. Talk to conservation professionals as well as to members of existing conservation groups to get more information. Their perspectives will help you decide if a need really does exist for your group and how best to fill it. Your research will also give you insight about potential sources of support for (and resistance to) your efforts.

PRACTICAL POINTERS

In this initial assessment process, it is important to:

1. Work to gather reliable and complete information that represents all perspectives and not just the favorable ones.

2. Honestly review this information while weighing the pros and cons of encouraging a grassroots effort.

3. Remember that professional and considerate behavior on the part of the group's representatives at this time will go a long way toward furthering the cause of your grassroots organization.

With the area's unmet needs clearly in mind, begin to consider the niche your new group might best fill. Although clearly identifying this distinct and compelling mission is essential, it may take several projects or even a full season or two before the group is able to refine and agree upon its "true" mission. Don't worry. Going into the early projects with only a broad understanding of what the group is all about allows the early leaders to help shape, and therefore share, the ownership of the vision. (Mission statements are discussed in more detail in the next chapter—see page 46.)

Cultivate Community Support

Identifying a clear need for your organization and deciding on its mission and focus are only the first steps in creating a successful organization. A real need for a grassroots conservation effort doesn't necessarily ensure an enthusiastic welcome by the community. The reception an organization's efforts will receive, now and in the future, depends on cultivating local support from other volunteer groups, political and business figures, the media, and land managers. A volunteer group with the enthusiastic backing of the community is much more likely to survive the inevitable financial, political, and personnel crises that come as an organization grows and matures. Some ways of cultivating local support for an organization include:

Find an Insider. In any community, there are some individuals who have the respect of almost everyone. These insiders have immediate access to community leaders and know the ins and outs of the local scene. Discussing ideas with an insider first will save many steps in collecting information and "taking the temperature" of the community. You can learn a lot simply by listening to an insider, getting his or her perspective on how conservation fits into the community as a whole. An insider can also open many doors that might otherwise be closed. Support by an insider lends immediate credibility to a group's mission and to the organization itself. Possible insiders include city mayors, respected conservationists, local politicians, business leaders, and agency heads.

PRACTICAL POINTERS

1. Document contacts. Keep records of the whos, whats, whens, and wheres of visits. These records will become a crucial reference and guide.

2. Follow up contacts with a thank-you letter. Busy people will appreciate this professional behavior. This letter is also a good way to reiterate important parts of a conversation and to get verbal agreements down on paper. Copies of these letters are important documentation for funding and agency support.

Create Your Own Turf and Respect Others' Turf. One sure way to win someone's enmity is to step on their toes. As information is gathered about the need and support for the group's efforts, pay attention to how possible activities might threaten or possibly undermine those of other groups. Seek out opportunities to demonstrate how the group can create its own niche. Show that it will not "steal" resources or opportunities from someone else.

Listen and Learn. There is no point in repeating the mistakes of others. Use their insights and experiences as guides. Ask questions of experienced people to see what went right and what went wrong for them.

Develop Ownership. The more individuals and groups can play a role in shaping the agenda of a new group, the more they feel that they have a stake in its survival and success. Give all key players (other volunteer groups, agency heads, etc.) a chance to help shape and "own" the group's agenda. Their ideas and experience will only help to create a better product, and their long-term support is crucial.

Create a Steering Committee

Obviously, one person does not make an organization. In order to get things going, many people need to help. A temporary steering committee (the nucleus of an eventual board of directors) is the beginning of an organization that will endure. During the first season, the steering committee has two important functions. The first is to provide the energy and personnel to organize and complete a few visible hands-on projects. The second is to increase the organization's support and credibility in the community.

One way to create a steering committee is to invite contacts made during the assessment phase to an informational/organizational meeting. At this meeting, present your assessment of the conservation needs and the initial strategy for meeting those needs through action-oriented projects. After you have presented your assessment and strategy, recruit five to seven participants at the meeting to serve on an initial steering committee to organize first projects.

PRACTICAL POINTERS

1. Use the group's insider as a spokesperson at this meeting. An insider's credibility and understanding of local politics is important here.

2. Create an opportunity for an open discussion where participants can ask questions and raise objections. Give others a chance to champion ideas, as well as to modify them and present their own.

3. Keep the focus on the limited, concrete tasks of organizing a steering committee and getting a first project started. Although it is important to inspire and motivate people by talking about long-term needs and goals, try to stick to the topic. The group will be off to a better start if it remains organized and focused from the beginning, doing one thing at a time.

■ ■ ■

Cultivate Financial Support

Most fledgling grassroots organizations need some financial support, if only to cover the costs of mailing, telephone calls, photocopying, etc. If the scope of the organization's initial activities is fairly modest, this support may come in the form of donations from interested volunteers. For more extensive efforts (and particularly if the organization needs the help of a paid staff person), securing seed money is a must.

Meet with community leaders, foundation executives, agency staff, and local business people to explore the possibility of seed grants. Be sure not to get ahead of the steering committee during these exploratory meetings. Discuss the mission and planned activities of your organization and ask if funds might be available to help launch the organization. Possible sources of seed money are:

Local or Regional Foundations. Many foundations, particularly community-based ones, are receptive to making grants to start new local groups that meet local needs. (Businesses are a possibility but generally give smaller amounts to established organizations. They will be important sources of funds later on).

Government Agencies. Contracts and cooperative agreements with government agencies for your new organization to perform specific services or projects can be important sources of seed money. The agency must be convinced that the group's volunteers will be able to deliver before they will commit funds. The group's "insider," documentation of the successes of similar groups, or an initial unreimbursed all-volunteer project may be helpful in making your case. State (and particularly local) agencies often have more flexibility to enter into such sole-source contracts, memoranda of understanding, and fee-for-service arrangements than federal agencies. For instance, in Colorado, a memo of understanding with a state agency allowed Volunteers for Outdoor Colorado to hire and pay its first staff person for two years. In return, VOC conducted a series of volunteer tree-planting projects on reclaimed strip mines. This gave VOC the time it needed to develop a large dedicated group of volunteers and other, more stable, sources of income.

Volunteer groups often work together with the U.S. Forest Service and other government agencies to share in a project's costs and labor.

In many cases, federal funding in the form of a "challenge cost share" can be secured through the U.S.D.A. Forest Service and similar programs with other federal agencies. The Forest Service's "challenge cost share" gives public and private organizations the opportunity to work cooperatively with the Forest Service to form partnerships to work on projects that benefit the national forests. Each partner contributes to the cost of the project in the form of cash, materials, services, or labor. There is no formal application process. Organizations with good ideas merely contact their local Forest Service Office.

If seed money is not available, all is not lost. Proceed at a slower pace. Run fewer projects but make each one even better. At the end of a successful project season, go back to initial funding prospects, and others, and point to the group's recent success. Prove that the idea and approach are worthy of their support and give these prospects another chance to "get in on the ground floor" during the second season.

Sponsor Hands-On, Action-oriented Projects

These projects are the lifeblood of a fledgling grassroots organization. They provide both the focus and the fun and are the best way to recruit new members. Volunteers at a project not only accomplish a task but also learn about the group's goals and vision. With good follow-up, some volunteers may be persuaded to become project leaders, committee chairs, or board members. If they have fun at one project, they are likely to return with their friends and families to work on another one.

It is important that first projects be:

- Fun and rewarding for volunteers.

- Successful. This creates a positive first impression and builds lasting credibility.

- Highly visible and well publicized. This increases exposure and community support.

- Manageable. Fifty to 150 volunteers for a day are plenty to start with.

- Clearly committed to quality. Quality is important in motivating volunteers and building credibility with agencies and the community.

- Ambitious, but achievable. Looking back over a hard job, well done, can be a tremendous source of pride and motivation.

- Clearly useful. Make-work projects kill the motivation of quality volunteers.
- Well supervised by the planning group.

Examples of good first projects are:

- Repairing a major erosion problem at a highly used local park.
- Planting trees or shrubs in a relatively concentrated area.
- Constructing trails.
- Repairing a seriously damaged, but very popular, trail.
- Sponsoring a trek to explore the feasibility of a potential trail or greenway corridor.

A trail maintenance day is an excellent action-oriented first project for a conservation group.

- Removing airplane wreckage from a visible spot in a popular wilderness area.
- Spearheading an extensive cleanup and rehabilitation of a river or popular park.
- Removing ugly, non-native vines choking vegetation at a popular park.
- Removing major graffiti.
- Repairing erosion at a boating access site.
- Removing abandoned buildings from a natural area.

Note: These projects have all been successfully accomplished by grassroots conservation organizations.

Examples of projects to avoid are:

- Litter pickups. They are common, unexciting and the litter often returns quickly.
- Minor trail maintenance.
- Anything dangerous or hazardous.
- Anything that spreads participants out so far that they can't enjoy each others' company.
- Anything too controversial (especially during the first year).

PRACTICAL POINTERS

1. Assign and train project leaders in advance. Training should include on-site work experience in the actual activities they will lead. A mandatory two- to three- hour training session for leaders on the Thursday evening before a Saturday project works well.

2. Worker-to-leader ratio varies with the project. However, it should never exceed ten to one.

3. Make it possible for everyone to eat lunch together. Social interaction is very important.

4. Give participants the opportunity to change jobs at lunchtime if they wish.

5. Remember to document all projects with photographs and videotape. These will be useful for future recruiting and fund-raising and will make valuable archival material decades from now.

Timetable for Planning and Running a Successful Project

The timetable for organizing your first project depends on its scope and your objectives. Smaller projects or ones for which you already have a leader and about which you already have a great deal of knowledge and expertise may be organized fairly quickly. Others require more lead time.

The following is a basic schedule for running a project that covers the essential activities. Depending on your organization, your project, and the availability of skilled volunteers, some of these activities may be more or less important and take more or less time. Remember that your primary goal is not to follow a particular schedule, but to run a good project. Use this timetable as a checklist to help you cover the necessary bases, not as an absolute. To run a project on July 1, use these dates as guidelines:

- February 1: Set project goals (e.g., recruit volunteer leaders and workers, begin to develop broad name recognition [publicity], accomplish much needed work.)

- February and March: Research prospective projects

- April 1: Select project and appoint volunteer project coordinator

- April 15: Develop time line, identify specific tasks, and delegate responsibilities for tasks. Typical tasks include: scouting the area to estimate volunteers and crews needed; recruiting leaders, volunteers, and a master of ceremonies for project day; publicity; training leaders; gathering tools and materials.

- May and June: Monitor and assist with tasks
- June 1: Send out first press release
- June 15: Send out second press release
- June 25: Leader training (best to have this on the Wednesday evening before a Saturday project or on the Saturday before if the work will be particularly sophisticated)
- July 1: Project day
- July 1 through 7: Thank participants by telephone, mail, and/or in person and invite them to the next Steering Committee meeting.
- July 10: Hold follow-up Steering Committee meeting. Evaluate project and begin planning the next one.

Recruit and Integrate Volunteers Identified through Projects

The primary purpose of early public service projects is to increase the organization's credibility and to recruit high-quality volunteers to serve as organizational leaders. The influx of new energy from these volunteers makes it possible to build and sustain the organization. Recruiting these volunteers into the organization, however, takes planning, thought, and effort.

Everyone involved in an organization is a potential recruiter. Expect all members to talk to outsiders about the organization. Require project leaders to be responsible for getting to know all of their crew members and for identifying those who might be good for future projects and leadership roles in the organization.

PRACTICAL POINTERS

1. Use the "5 percent rule." Recruit at least 5 percent of the new volunteers at each project into active leadership positions in the organization.

2. Keep an accurate list of all project participants including name, address, and phone number.

3. Make sure that all project leaders and key volunteers assume responsibility for recruiting new leaders and new members during the projects and see this effort as a priority. Each project leader should make a personal thank-you/invitation phone call to all of his/her crew members within ten days of the project.

4. End a project with a social event (e.g., dance, barbecue, picnic). This is a fun reward for the volunteers' efforts and provides an opportunity to personally encourage the best volunteers to attend a follow-up Steering Committee meeting.

Remember that projects are recruiting tools. Take the opportunity at the project to get to know individual volunteers, to pass out literature, and to make announcements.

Hold a follow-up Steering Committee meeting within two weeks of the project. Encourage the best volunteers from the project to attend by announcing the meeting at the project, mailing out agendas, and calling volunteers personally. Start this meeting with a slide show of the project and token or humorous awards to participants as a way to recapture the energy, fun, and enthusiasm of the project day. Make sure to involve everyone (especially new recruits) in planning and committing to the next project. Give new recruits formal roles on the Steering Committee or in organizing the next project. Encourage new volunteers to recruit their friends for the next project.

Build Single Projects into a Program of Ongoing Public Service

The first project season will undoubtedly be hectic. Initial projects may be diverse and seem somewhat unrelated. But remember that they will help to recruit new members, increase credibility, and help the group refine its vision/mission.

When planning for the future, focus on the most successful past projects. Plan similar projects, or annual follow-ups to past projects, to create a core program that will help to identify and to define the organization. Continuing projects (e.g., user education programs) are also a good way to establish a core program around which other efforts can be focused.

PRACTICAL POINTER

1. Whenever possible, delegate ongoing responsibility for core projects to the volunteers most committed to these projects in the past.

Use these core projects as a way to maintain the group's momentum and identity as it tackles longer term organizational issues. Help members to see the relationship between dealing with these long-term issues and the group's ability to sponsor fun and useful projects.

Example: Volunteers for Outdoor Colorado (VOC)

In March 1982, the AMC's National Volunteer Project (NVP) representatives met the Director of the Colorado Office of Volunteerism at a national conference. She felt there was a need for organized outdoor volunteerism in Colorado and that the state would be very supportive of an effort to start such a program. She urged the NVP to select Colorado as a demonstration area. That fall, the NVP met with government agencies and outdoor organizations in Colorado. These contacts confirmed her prediction of need and support in the state.

In April 1983, the NVP and Colorado Office of Volunteerism called a meeting of government agencies, outdoor organizations, and businesses to discuss the concept further and to develop strategies. The group was enthusiastic and designated a six-person Steering Committee to pursue the project with the NVP. The Steering Committee selected the name Colorado Public Lands Council and developed a very ambitious plan for a joint statewide volunteer and outdoor recreation information center. It spent the next twelve months attempting to secure $250,000 in seed money to fund it. In retrospect, this was a mistake. An entire project season was wasted and several eager volunteer leaders drifted away because there were no tangible outlets for their energies.

In early 1984, the Steering Committee changed its strategy. They changed their name to Volunteers for Outdoor Colorado (VOC) and developed plans for hands-on projects. They raised $700 from Denver businesses and formed a partnership with the Colorado Mined Land Reclamation Division (MLRD), a state agency. VOC and MLRD entered into a contract that committed VOC to run a series of volunteer tree planting projects on reclaimed strip mines in return for approximately $40,000. VOC used the funds to hire a thirty-hour-per-week coordinator in July 1984. This seed grant covered nearly all of VOC's operating expenses for two years.

By the end of 1984, VOC had run four projects involving 225 volunteers. During the winter, VOC established its first formal board of directors (thirteen directors), incorporated, and filed for tax-exempt status.

In 1985, VOC established a paying membership and registered 350 members by year's end. They sponsored six projects involving 555 volunteers that year, including one weekend when 200 volunteers planted 6,000 native trees and shrubs on a reclaimed strip mine. By the end of 1986, VOC had built a board of directors and developed strong independent volunteer committees. VOC's volunteer fundraisers had been successful enough to allow the group to hire an office manager—their second staff person. VOC was well on its way to becoming a leader in conservation.

By 1990, VOC's success had been honored with numerous awards, including the President's Take Pride in America Award for outstanding achievement in conserving America's natural and cultural resources in 1987, 1989, and 1990. By the end of 1991, VOC had 1,500

Hands-on land reclamation projects with visible results are satisfying and useful outlets for volunteer energy.

paying members and a staff of six. More important, they had involved over 11,000 volunteers in 52 hands-on projects making improvements to Colorado's public land worth an estimated $1.2 million.

VOC is a good example of a strong, successful organization based on rewarding hands-on projects. By recognizing early mistakes and redirecting its efforts toward highly visible and achievable volunteer actions, the group built on simple beginnings to become a large and vigorous organization. Even as it grew, VOC continued to focus on its primary tasks: volunteer-centered projects that had an immediate, positive effect on the environment. How to create and manage an organization's growth is the subject of the next chapter.

Phase Two

Organizational Development

A FIRST SEASON of successful projects builds credibility, increases visibility, and helps a grassroots conservation organization to further define its purpose. But most important, the first project season recruits a core of committed leaders and members into the organization. The advent of the organization's second season raises new issues. Now is the time for members to decide how (and if) to tackle organizational issues such as a mission statement, the organizational structure, fund-raising and membership development, and long-range planning.

This phase of an organization's development poses particular challenges. It requires careful balancing of organizational nitty-gritty with the need to continue action-oriented projects. Too often at this stage, organizational development drains time and energy away from hands-on projects. To keep the right focus, it is particularly important to manage organizational issues in ways that are concrete, specific, and contribute to the group's overall conservation effort.

Creating an ongoing organizational structure often requires an influx of new leaders. Many project-oriented leaders will find the nuts-and-bolts work of building a solid organization tedious and unrewarding. However, others will understand the need for organizational development and will enjoy working on these challenges to help accomplish the organization's mission.

Again, organizational development will go most smoothly if the group stays focused on its primary task: action-oriented conservation projects. Fund-raising, mission statements, membership drives, etc., are done to enhance the group's ability to accomplish its primary task, and not for their own sake.

The next section presents a brief overview of topics related to organizational development. Some topics may be immediately relevant to your organization while others may not. It is important to remember that successful grass-roots conservation organizations come in many shapes and sizes with varying levels of formal organizational development. Use these sections as an outline for consideration, not as a set of rules that you must follow. Additional references on each topic are listed in the appendices to help you build a usable and accessible reference library on topics important to the group.

PRACTICAL POINTERS

1. In the first year, keep the group focused on action through accomplishing projects. If a few individuals are interested in organizational issues and structure early in the start-up phase, this is fine. Clearly define a task and let them get started. The important thing is to make sure that early attention to these issues does not bog the group down.

2. In the second year, maintain the project focus while addressing relevant organizational development issues. The litmus test for relevance is whether addressing the issue will substantially improve the organization's ability to accomplish its mission.

3. Use a **two-meeting approach** to discuss and approve important documents and plans. For example, have a single author or small committee prepare a draft in advance and mail it to the Steering Committee or board. Discuss the draft and entertain revisions at the first meeting. Then refer it back to the authors for revision. The amended version can be presented and approved at the next meeting.

4. Whenever possible, at least 50 percent of the slots on the developing organizational chart should be filled by leaders well grounded in the group's core projects.

▪▪▪

Mission Statement, Goals, and Objectives

The mission statement and statements of goals and objectives are simple, short, written statements that guide the organization and all its efforts. They help the group create and maintain its clear, compelling vision; evaluate the success of past activities; and plan for the future. Although these statements are the most important parts of any planning process, they are too often written quickly, filed, and never seen again. The group then runs the risk of becoming the proverbial "ship without a rudder." Therefore, it is important to put some effort into creating these guiding statements.

The Mission Statement. A mission statement should clearly state what the **organization is all about** and what important single purpose it serves. It should be broad enough to accommodate different approaches but specific enough to distinguish the group from others and motivate those who read it. The following is a good example:

The mission of Volunteers for Outdoor Colorado is to instill in Coloradans a sense of personal responsibility for their public lands resulting in beneficial stewardship of the state's natural resources.

Be sure to capture the essence of what the group wants to accomplish. Is "building and maintaining the XYZ Trail" all there is to it, or is "building opportunities for adventure, mystery, wilderness experience, family togetherness, etc." through the trail an important aspect of what the group is all about? If so, include it in the mission statement.

Goals. A group should agree on and write down no more than three or four goals that describe **specific ways to accomplish** the mission during the next three to five years. The following examples of goals refer to the previous mission statement:

1. To involve Coloradans in constructive projects to improve public lands and natural resources.
2. To increase the sense of responsibility Coloradans feel for their public lands.
3. To increase the ability of Coloradans to participate knowledgeably in land management decisions and policy making.

Objectives. Objectives are **very specific measurable statements** that refer to specific goals. A good objective for the first goal above would be:

> In 1987, the group will complete three tree planting projects and four trail maintenance projects, each involving at least 100 volunteers.

When developing objectives, make sure there is a specific committee or individual that will be responsible for each objective, from the planning and thinking process through completion. Hold them accountable for their objective.

PRACTICAL POINTERS

1. Immediately following the first season of projects, ask the group's two most visionary (but realistic) members to draft a mission statement and goals for the organization. Use past project experience as a basis for creating and evaluating these drafts.

2. Use the two-meeting approach (see page 45) to refine and approve the mission, goals, and objectives.

3. When the mission, goals, and objectives have been accepted and approved, write them down and refer to them regularly at meetings, in publications, and in publicity. All organization members should develop and carry out their programs with these statements clearly in mind.

4. Make sure all of the organization's leaders can state the mission. No group can accomplish its mission if the leaders don't clearly understand and agree on what the mission is. Periodically, someone should surprise leaders by asking them to write down the organization's purpose from memory. Then, hand out copies of the mission statement so they can see if they were on target.

5. Review and update the mission, goals, and objectives annually. If there is a shift in focus, make sure everyone understands it.

■ ■ ■

Organizational Structure

For many people, organizational structure conjures up diagrams of formal reporting relationships, visions of endless red tape, and the death of fun and spontaneity. The purpose of setting up a structure in a grassroots conservation organization is to create an environment that facilitates getting things done, not one that slows things down and consumes precious volunteer energy. The focus of the organization should still be on action to accomplish its mission. Any structure developed by the organization should reflect that mission and support that action. Here are some practical specifics about typical organizational structures.

Board of Directors. The board makes all the important decisions for the organization. It is the brain, the conscience, and the command center. An effective board can open up opportunities in the community, focus the organization to accomplish its mission, and inspire and lead members. Ineffective boards can be overbearing, become isolated from the membership, and stagnate the group into oblivion with unnecessary red tape. It all depends on who the directors are and on how their jobs are defined. Some things to consider when setting up a board include:

1. *Size.* A five- to twelve-member board usually allows for a broad representation of the membership but is still small enough to act quickly if necessary.
2. *Membership.* Avoid restrictions that require that certain directors come from certain constituencies (e.g., two from government agencies, two from the northern region, two canoeing members, etc.). This will

tie the hands of the nominating committee and lead to power struggles on the board. All directors should have the overall best interest of the organization at heart, not that of a certain constituency within the organization.

3. *Mix of Members.* Avoid the temptation to recruit either a "heavy hitter" board or a "working" board. Boards between these two extremes usually work the best. Some board members should be drawn from the ranks of the proven project leaders who continue to get their hands dirty on projects. Some should be well connected in the community and may focus on raising funds or establishing connections with other organizations. Try some of the following places when searching for directors (and officers):

   - Leaders identified and developed through the projects.
   - Management of corporations where the group's volunteers work.
   - The group's government agency partners.
   - Prominent outdoors people.
   - Managers from organizations being solicited for funds.
   - Other outdoor organizations.

4. *Responsibilities and Commitments.* Four to six meetings per year for the full board interspersed with executive committee meetings works very well. With more meetings, burnout becomes a serious concern. With fewer meetings, the board lacks necessary information and begins to feel ineffective.

PRACTICAL POINTERS

1. Create a job description for directors so that they know what they are being asked to do before they make a commitment to serve. This will also force the group to define the scope of the job before serious recruiting begins.

2. Have an orientation for directors and give them an orientation packet including the mission statement, the organization's history, its articles of incorporation and bylaws, a summary of the board's responsibilities, a board membership list, and specific job descriptions for various board positions. The *Board Manual Workbook* by Stringer is a useful guide to creating an effective orientation package (see Appendices).

3. Provide directors with enough background to make intelligent decisions.

4. Create an executive committee. It is essentially a subcommittee of the board and is often made up of the officers or the president and important committee heads. Within certain parameters, the executive committee can meet between regular board meetings and act on behalf of the board.

▪ ▪ ▪

Selecting Officers. The people filling the positions of chairperson (or president), vice-chair, secretary, and treasurer are the most important in the organization. Selecting the right people term after term is crucial. It takes time and energy but is always worth the investment. Never select "Old Joe" because "it's his turn and no one else will do it."

It is important to make sure that candidates are qualified. Consider these criteria when selecting candidates for chairperson and vice-chairperson. Is the candidate:

- ▪ A good manager and delegator with "people skills?"
- ▪ Sympathetic to the cause and supportive of the group's mission?
- ▪ Familiar with the group's efforts?
- ▪ Acceptable to a majority of group's other leaders and members?
- ▪ Willing to make a substantial time commitment?
- ▪ A recognizable name in the community?

Admittedly, this is a tall order and very few candidates will get a perfect score on every criteria. But remember, time spent now finding the right directors and officers will pay off in the long run.

Try to allow for staggered two-year terms for directors and officers. This will provide continuity by assuring that the entire board does not turn over in a single term and will give directors enough time to make a substantial impact without requiring an immense time commitment (over two years). Also, conduct "exit interviews" with outgoing officers and directors and have them revise (or create) the job descriptions for their replacements. This will add continuity and ensure that any duties that "fell" to the position will be included in the new description if appropriate.

PRACTICAL POINTERS

1. Designate a two- to four-person nominating committee to draw up the slate of candidates for board and officer positions to be voted on at the first and subsequent annual meetings.

2. Get the right people in the right places. Interview candidates before they are nominated. Ask them what they are interested in and make sure that they have the skills necessary to do the job. It makes no sense to elect a Treasurer that doesn't understand (or want to learn about) budgets. Use the interview to present an honest picture of what the job entails. Everyone will be unhappy if the wrong person ends up in the wrong position.

3. After agreeing on the criteria for officers (and directors), the nominating committee should put together a list of "ideal" candidates numbered in order of preference. The two leaders most familiar with each candidate should meet with the candidate in order to ask him/her to serve. Have a backup request ("Would you serve as a publicity consultant for us if you are too busy to serve on the board?") if they decline. Even if they are not willing to serve on the board, they may agree to help in other ways. Don't be afraid to go after several prominent candidates. Follow up and stay in touch with these people, even if they can't help immediately.

4. Sit down with each incoming leader and help him/her set two or three realistic goals to tackle during the term.

Committees help an organization meet its action-oriented goals. They exist to serve projects, not as ends in themselves.

Committees. Projects, publicity, fund-raising, membership, finance, nominating, and planning are crucial functions that will help the organization to meet its goals. But don't assume that each will require an entire committee. Remember that the structure must serve the projects and not the other way around. If planning occurs at an annual board retreat, a planning committee may not be needed. If there are two people who love publicity and get the work done well but don't want to serve on a committee, fine. Don't call them a committee! The important point is that those responsible for each function know clearly what to do and get it done.

In order to ensure effective committees and working groups, use job descriptions for each committee or committee function. Meet with each committee to set annual

PRACTICAL POINTER

1. Managing Committees. The board chairperson
   and, to a lesser extent, the staff person (if any)
   are responsible for monitoring and motivating
   committee heads. They should meet with and
   call the committee heads at least every month.
   These regular meetings and/or telephone calls
   are the most important management function
   in the organization. They are a chance to
   exchange information, check on progress, and
   give moral support. Make sure this responsibility is clearly understood and carried out.

goals. Remember to write these goals down and to hold individuals accountable for achieving them.

Chapters. The preceding discussion of organizational structure addressed issues that arise early in the development of most grassroots conservation organizations. Groups having a broad geographic focus and those experiencing steady growth must eventually decide whether or not to establish chapters. Decentralizing the group's structure through chapters can offer advantages. Local responsiveness, friendly competition among chapters, access to local resources, and local pride, recognition and control may all be improved by establishing autonomous chapters. When considering this type of structure, it is essential to establish a clear definition of the authority and responsibility of both the chapters and the central organization. Other crucial issues are the allocation of dues money and access to funding sources.

Articles of Incorporation/Bylaws

Eventually, every grassroots conservation organization must decide whether or not to incorporate. A corporation is a legal entity recognized by the state to carry out specific purposes and organized to meet legal requirements of that state. Although composed of a group of individuals, the corporation is legally regarded as distinct from its members. Some groups may decide that incorporation is unnecessarily cumbersome and does not substantially contribute to getting the job done. Others find that incorporation is the only way to accomplish their mission. Here are some of the factors to weigh when considering incorporation:

Advantages

1. *Ability to Receive Funding.* Form follows funding. To accept charitable contributions from people or corporations that want to receive income tax benefits, an organization must be designated as tax-exempt under certain IRS codes. To get such a designation, the group must be incorporated.

2. *Liability Protection for Members.* The laws governing an unincorporated association make it difficult to view it as a legal entity apart from the people involved. Incorporation may help protect the members of the organization from personal liability when they act on behalf of the organization. However, organizers must get legal advice on the extent of the protection offered by incorporation and explore other means of protecting individuals from liability if the organization doesn't incorporate.

3. *Organizational Stability.* Incorporation allows the organization the flexibility to enter into contracts

and cooperative agreements, have a bank account, and accept certain kinds of funding. This also helps to provide stability and continuity for the group. The organization's existence doesn't rely on the participation of any one individual who has signed the contract or opened the bank account.

Disadvantages

For any group whose vision for itself extends beyond the next twelve months, the disadvantages of incorporation are few. Undecided groups should consider using an established organization as a short-term umbrella to address funding and liability issues.

1. *Incorporation Takes (Some) Time.* Incorporation can be (but doesn't need to be) time and energy consuming. It takes time initially to meet the legal requirements for incorporation. In addition, incorporated organizations must file yearly statements in order to maintain their status. Preparing the appropriate documents and making sure they are filed on a timely basis requires effort. Having someone in the organization with legal expertise will make this easier.

2. *Incorporation Requires (Some) Structure.* An incorporated organization necessitates a more formal structure (at least on paper). Certain roles (for example, president, secretary, and treasurer) must be created and filled. It may be harder psychologically (although not much harder legally) to disband or change an incorporated organization once it has served its purpose than it is to disband or change a less formal organization.

The most important factor to consider when thinking about incorporation is whether it helps the organization do its work more effectively. If the answer is yes, read on.

The *Articles of Incorporation* is a four- to six-page legal document that sets forth the purpose of the organization, where it will do business, and, in a broad way, how it will be run. It is important to give attention to the organization's formal statement of purpose early on when putting together the incorporation documents. The statement of purpose must qualify as an "exempt purpose" if 501(c)(3) status will eventually be sought. ("Exempt purposes" include charitable, literary, scientific, or educational activities, the prevention of cruelty to children and animals, testing for public safety, and fostering national or international amateur sports competition.)

The *bylaws* often run six to eight pages in length and are much more detailed. They set forth the specific rules that will govern meetings and organizational affairs, including how the board and officers will be elected, the powers of the board and membership, minimum numbers of meetings, and so on.

Both the Articles of Incorporation and the bylaws are important legal documents that must be in proper order. A lawyer or person experienced with such documents should review them to make sure they are complete and conform to the standards of the state in which the organization will operate. Such a review can help make the process quick and painless.

PRACTICAL POINTERS

1. Borrow copies of Articles and bylaws from other local nonprofit groups. These have already passed the legal tests of the state. Use them as models if their owners are happy with them, but be sure to tailor them to fit the needs of your own organization.

2. Contact the state's Office of Volunteerism, the United Way, community foundations, or local nonprofit assistance services. They will be able to help with the incorporation process or will suggest others who can.

3. Check to see if one of the group's members is (or knows) an attorney who could help with details. Check also to see if anyone in the group has been involved with incorporating another group.

▪▪▪

Filing for Tax-Exempt Status

The incorporation process previously described occurs at the state level. The tax-exempt process is a federal one through the IRS. The objective is to become a 501(c)3 organization. This will exempt the group from paying federal income tax and allow any contributions to the group to be deducted from the donor's taxable income. If the group plans to raise money by donations or grants, this classification is *essential.*

It is much easier to raise funds after the organization has received its IRS "determination letter" making it tax-exempt. Many foundations and corporations won't even consider requests for contributions until then. However, the group may raise funds before receiving its "determination letter" if the fund-raisers are completely up-front about the group's status. Be honest with contacts or they might permanently disappear.

The actual application is the IRS Kit 1023 and supplemental information that the group must provide. The form focuses on identification, purpose, activities, operational details, and detailed financial records. Be sure to get IRS Publication 557 "Tax-Exempt Status for Your Organization," which explains in detail how to properly complete the 1023.

To complete the tax-exempt process will take from three to six months after incorporation. Remember that the same people or groups that helped with incorporation will be useful resources for the tax-exempt process. Also, try to get assistance completing the IRS forms, if possible. Mistakes or omissions can seriously delay the application process.

STAGES TO TAX-EXEMPT STATUS

I. Articles of Incorporation   **Bylaws**
  (Internal Document)   (Internal Document)

II. Incorporation (State procedure)

III. Tax-exempt status 501(c)(3) (Federal procedure)

PRACTICAL POINTERS

1. To facilitate early fund-raising, apply for an "advance ruling" of tax exemption with the IRS. The procedure and details are in Publication 557.

2. Calling the regional IRS office and talking to the people who are reviewing the application may help. Having a personal contact can sometimes accelerate things.

3. Keep complete and accurate financial records from the very beginning. This will make it much easier to complete the IRS Form 1023 when the time comes.

4. The publication *Starting a Land Trust* by the Land Trust Alliance provides an excellent overview of the essential elements in the setting up and development of land trusts and is highly applicable to grassroots conservation organizations in their early stages.

5. All IRS forms and kits may be obtained through a toll-free order number: (800)829-3676.

▪ ▪ ▪

Planning

Thoughtful planning is crucial to the success of the organization. It helps the group decide where it is going and lets it know when it gets there. Planning can also be easy and fun. For instance, deciding what projects to do next is an important and exciting form of planning.

Once your grassroots organization gets off the ground, you may want to try a variation of the following timetable:

▪ September: board reviews and revises the previous year's activities, reviews the mission and goals, and tentatively approves specific objectives (and, if possible, actual projects to meet these objectives) for the following year.

▪ October: All committees meet to evaluate their performance for the season just completed and to develop written strategies with budgets that will allow them to accomplish their portions of the overall plan drafted in September. This includes tentatively selecting the following season's projects.

▪ November: Executive Committee prepares an overall budget and plan for the following year using the committee strategies.

▪ December: board reviews and approves the plan and budget for the following year.

▪ January: Annual Meeting—Board and officers elected.

▪ January—August: Implement overall plan.

Planning for the organization should be an ongoing process that involves these components:

- Assessing needs.

- Identifying the most important needs and ranking them in order of importance.

- Developing alternative strategies for meeting those needs.

- Choosing a strategy.

- Implementing the strategy.

- Evaluation of all programs and progress toward goals and objectives.

PRACTICAL POINTER

1. Choose most of the next year's projects during the early stages of the planning process. This will give plenty of lead time to organize, publicize, and raise funds for them. It will also maintain the project focus throughout the planning process. Leave a few project slots open, however, to allow for last minute opportunities and spontaneity.

Finances

Whether or not the organization plans to hire paid staff or carry out expensive programs, managing finances is important. Sloppy bookkeeping or inadequate planning and budgeting drains enthusiasm and energy away from more important issues, such as having fun doing projects.

In order to manage finances :
- Recruit a competent treasurer. Look among yourselves for the best and most willing numbers person. Ask other organizations for referrals. Contact business associations and civic clubs. Many financial professionals are active in outdoor and conservation activities and would be willing to serve if asked.

- Agree to budget categories that will be reviewed, then monitored by the treasurer. Sample budget categories might include: telephone, postage, insurance, salaries.

- Set up a record-keeping system that is consistent with accepted accounting practices.

- Monitor the budget and make adjustments in spending or income generation if necessary.

- Make sure large checks require more than one signature.

The key to good budgeting is to identify categories that work for your organization and allow you to evaluate progress toward accomplishing organizational goals. Program budgeting is excellent in this regard since it breaks down all line item costs according to program initiatives. This allows the organization to track all expenses and revenues associated with each of its project efforts.

On the facing page is a sample budget. This budget is generally representative of a young organization (two to three years old) that has advanced to the point where they now have a half-time staff person and 250 dues-paying members (dues of $20/year).

PROGRAM BUDGET

Expenditures (Program Areas/Goals)

LINE ITEM	Trail Days	Fish Ladder	Tree Planting	Fund-raising	Outreach	Totals
Salaries	3,000	2,000	2,000	1,500	1,500	10,000
Benefits	450	300	300	225	225	1,500
Insurance	210	140	140	105	105	700
Rent	1,080	720	720	540	540	3,600
Telephone	100	100	100	150	150	600
Printing	250	250	250	250	1,000	2,000
Postage	125	125	125	125	500	1,000
Tools/Equip.	100	200	200	—	—	500
Supplies	100	200	100	50	50	500
Totals	5,415	4,035	3,935	2,945	4,070	20,400

Revenues (Program Areas/Goals)

	Trail Days	Fish Ladder	Tree Planting	Fund-raising	Outreach	Totals
Grants	5,000	2,000			2,000	9,000
Donations	500	500	500			1,500
Membership					5,000	5,000
Contracts		2,000	2,000			4,000
Fees/Sales					900	900
Totals	5,500	4,500	2,500	000	7,900	20,400

Budget Summary

	Trail Days	Fish Ladder	Tree Planting	Fund-raising	Outreach	Totals
Expenses	5,415	4,035	3,935	2,945	4,070	20,400
Revenues	5,500	4,500	3,500	000	7,900	20,400
Profit or (loss)	85	465	(435)	(2,945)	3,830	10,000

Fund-raising

Too often volunteer organizations approach fund-raising the way Mark Twain said people approach the weather: everybody talks about it, but nobody does anything about it. Raising money intimidates more people than any other activity in grassroots organizations. It shouldn't. If your organization needs money to accomplish what it does best, making a convincing case to potential funders should be viewed as an opportunity to publicize your good work and further your cause. Remember, though, that raising funds is only a means to the end. It's not an end in itself. Don't spend time and energy on fund-raising until your organization has a specific need for the money.

Fund-raising involves the following:

Planning

1. *Create an Annual Budget.* Find a realistic balance between being overly shy and overly optimistic. Both extremes cause problems when raising money.

2. *Include All Legitimate Overhead Charges.* Staff salaries, rent, utilities, postage, and telephone are all legitimate costs of providing a service. They must be included in the budget and all fund-raising targets.

Considering Sources

1. *Foundations.* Foundations generally give relatively large amounts of money but for short periods of time. They are good sources of early grants. Foundations often have rigid requirements such as giving grants only to 501(c)(3) nonprofits or only giving them to help the needy in a certain city. Foundations

and some corporations have funding cycles requiring you to plan ahead, sometimes as much as twelve months from application to actually receiving funds. Researching these requirements ahead of time will save you from approaching the wrong foundation.

2. *Corporations.* Corporations generally give smaller amounts than foundations but can often be approached for many years. They may require less paperwork than foundations. Corporations are also a rich source of volunteers and "in-kind" services such as printing, office support, space, and management consultation. You should actively court them for these, too.

3. *Individuals.* Over 90 percent of all charitable contributions made in the United States come from individuals. Donations range from a few dollars to many thousands. Standardize individual donations by establishing a paying membership program. However, even with a membership program, certain individual members and nonmembers should be contacted for specific donations.

4. *Contracts and Cooperative Agreements.* Some government agencies (and conceivably private businesses) will be willing to contract with your organization for a wide range of volunteer services. Examples include: managing campgrounds, building trails, planting trees, building fences, etc. Any service normally performed by the agency that the organization can provide at a lower cost is a possibility for a contract. Contracts can vary from large formal concessions with federal agencies to

handshake agreements on a fee-for-service basis with a local agency. Some may require extra insurance or even performance bonds. If contracts seem like a possibility, the group may want to give extra consideration to including the participation of agency staff as an informal advisor to the group or a non-voting board member. In general, agency staff will welcome the opportunity to participate as long as they feel there is no conflict of interest. In any case, make sure project choices are not made solely on the basis of potential income. Any contract should be for a project that would be undertaken even if no money were available.

Targeting Sources

1. *Ask the Board/Steering Committee.* They are obviously prospective sources of funds themselves and a source of other contacts. Everyone knows people who would be interested in funding the group's cause. An example of networking at its best is the work of eight board members from the Trail Center in California. They raised $1,500 in one evening by calling ten friends each during a phonathon for the center.

2. *Use a Library.* Most major libraries have a reference section devoted to charitable foundations and corporations. Call your local librarian. There will be national and often state directories of organizations that make contributions. These sources show you what groups make contributions to what types of organizations, the sizes of the grants they make, and how to apply. Using these resources can help you

focus on appropriate corporate and foundation prospects.

3. *Be Creative.* Remember that the large givers receive thousands of proposals each year. Don't overlook the local hardware store and smaller banks in favor of better known givers. Ask for help from established conservation groups in your region; you'll get good information and become part of the network of organizations in your area. Invite representatives from these groups to an informal brainstorming session about funding sources or possible leads. Consider the appeal your proposals may have to companies sharing the same regional focus, such as regional magazines, banks, or utilities. Seek advice from government agency staff about your projects and funding needs.

Soliciting Funds

1. *Write Proposals.* Some corporate and foundation prospects will have application forms and specific proposal requirements. Others will not. Any proposal should include an introduction, problem statement, a description of your organization, the organization's plan to address the problem, its needs (generally funds), a budget, and an appendix. Make sure the proposal makes a strong case for the need for the group's service and clearly shows why this group is in the best position to provide that service. The appendix should include such things as a list of board members with brief biographies, news clippings about the group's activities, and endorsement letters from well-known individuals. Include a one-

page cover letter outlining the high points of the proposal and making the specific request (e.g., $2,000 to support...). If possible, write your proposals on a computer. This allows you to tailor each proposal without retyping standard items that are included in all proposals. It is a good idea to call the prospects before sending a proposal to be sure the contact person and deadline are correct. This also alerts them that a request is on the way.

2. *Follow Up.* Call prospects within two weeks of sending the proposal to make sure it was received and to set up a meeting. The two leaders most familiar with the prospect should attend this meeting. The best situation is to have one of the volunteers who actually works at that company participate in the contact. Offer to clarify any points about the proposal and to discuss the organization and its plans. The most important thing to do, however, is to listen. The meeting may provide information that will enable you to strengthen the proposal or make a subsequent proposal more attractive to the donor.

Record Keeping

Much of fund-raising is developing relationships with the *people* who give the grants. The old saying that "people give to people, not to organizations" is very true. Record keeping is a crucial part of this. Start a file on each prospective funder and include notes from every meeting and phone conversation with them. Also be sure to keep an accurate prospect list that shows who is responsible for each prospect, the amount being requested, the contact person there, and the current status.

PRACTICAL POINTERS

1. When writing a proposal for a specific project, overhead can be included in two different ways. In the first, you add on a percentage (often 15 percent) of the direct costs of the project. In the second, you allocate a percentage of the total annual administrative overhead expense to the project. Base this percentage on the actual amount of time it will take to plan, carry out, and follow up the project.

2. Add funders and prospective funders to the mailing list and keep them informed about the program they supported. This is one more way to say thank-you. Never "take the money and run." Find creative ways to thank them, recognize them, and keep them informed.

3. Fund-raising is everyone's job, not just a committee's or a staff person's. Make sure all job descriptions reflect this. Make and keep fund-raising a priority for all group leaders. Be creative in thinking of all the group's activities as "fundable opportunities."

4. Ask for appropriate amounts. Don't ask the most generous prospect for only fifty dollars for tools. Knowing the appropriate amount depends on thorough research before your request.

5. Be persistent! The most creative work begins when the prospect says "no." Have backup requests and work to tailor a request to the prospect's interests and strengths (while being true to your organization's mission).

Hiring and Working with Paid Staff

Hiring and working with paid staff has its advantages and disadvantages. At its best, the relationship between an organization's volunteer leaders and its professional staff can be a picture of harmony and cooperation. At its worst, it can be a complete fiasco that threatens the organization's survival. Like any partnership, the relationships between volunteers and paid staff require constant care.

The first and most crucial choice is whether to hire professional staff in the first place. Hiring staff will change an all-volunteer organization, sometimes profoundly. Think about this change and what it might mean for the group. Careful planning is key. When thinking about the decision to hire professional staff, ask some of these questions. What

A paid staffer at work: Trail Coordinator Dave Sutton at The Trail Center, Palo Alto, California.

are the group's needs? What will they be six months or a year from now? Does our need to have someone to type and file today mean that we will need a secretary next summer? If professional help is needed, how much, and what kind? Does the group need a full-time executive director with a staff and budget to match, or would a part-time secretary with a desk and a phone do better?

To hire or not to hire? What can a professional staff do for the organization, and what are the potential pitfalls? Here are some of the advantages and disadvantages to consider:

Advantages

1. *More Freedom for Volunteers.* Staff can free up volunteer time by taking on responsibilities that the volunteer team may not have the enthusiasm or expertise to undertake.

2. *Continuity.* Staff can serve as a consistent communication center and provide continuity. Staff can usually spend many more hours on organizational affairs than can most volunteers and can manage comprehensive record keeping.

3. *Contact with the Community.* Having a consistent office presence during normal working hours can be a great advantage for contacts with agencies, prospective funders, media, etc.

4. *Better Decisions.* Good staff people can help an organization with decision making by offering a perspective on issues that is different from the volunteers'. They can also help decision makers avoid information overload by collecting and summarizing important information.

Disadvantages

1. *Expense.* Staff salaries are commonly the most expensive line item in a volunteer organization's budget. A half-time staffer with telephone, desk, and typewriter will cost approximately $25,000. Everyone must be prepared to work hard to fund any staff position once it is created.

2. *Possible Friction between Volunteers and Staff.* Hiring the right person for the group's needs, setting clear expectations, and communicating openly will minimize this possibility.

3. *"Creeping Professionalism."* This occurs when the staff grows faster than the participation of the volunteers they are there to serve. There is a fine line between a volunteer/staff partnership and overdependence on staff. Don't ignore the issue. Talk about it and plan for it. Above all, use the talents and energy of the staff to build volunteer capability, not replace it.

If the decision is made to hire a staff person, recruiting the right person is absolutely essential. Evaluate the organization's needs to determine what qualities and skills are needed. Would the group benefit most by hiring a field supervisor or an administrator, a leader or a follower, an eager novice or an experienced (and expensive) professional? Develop a comprehensive job description to help with this decision. Use this description to attract candidates and guide the successful candidate's performance.

Advertise professionally and broadly to attract quality applicants. This is an important and rewarding job. Don't sell it short by apologizing about aspects of the position or advertising by word-of-mouth only. Remember to involve experienced people in the hiring process. Interviewing is a skill most people feel they are very good at but few have actually mastered.

PRACTICAL POINTERS

1. Treat staff like the professionals they are. Set goals and formally review their performance every six months. Involve the group's most experienced personnel managers in this process.

2. Don't hire a staff person and expect him or her to "raise their own salary." The responsibility for fund-raising does not change when staff are hired. It still belongs to everyone, with the board still in the lead.

3. Actively involve staff in writing and revising their own job descriptions and in setting goals and performance standards.

4. The board of directors sets policy and hires the executive director who should have the primary responsibility for directing other staff (if any) according to those policies. In conjunction with setting the budget, the executive director and the board should determine the range of staff salary and benefits, allowing the executive director some discretion in this area.

■ ■ ■

Publicity

Publicity is crucial to accomplishing the mission of a grass-roots conservation organization. Getting the word out about who the group is, what it does, and how people can get involved is the only way the group can reach out and prosper. Publicity is particularly important for recruiting members and successful fund-raising. What your group does is news. All you must do is convince the local media of this fact. Doing this can be a lot easier than it might appear.

To get the best start on publicity, try to recruit the help of an experienced public relations person from the start. You may find a PR person among your volunteers, in a firm that employs one of your volunteers, or in a public agency with whom your organization works. You want a person with experience not because publicity is too hard for the layman to tackle; it's just that someone who knows

Publicity is the lifeblood of any long-term project. Signs, posters, and newsworthy events all contribute.

the local media comes with contacts that would take months or even years to develop.

However, remember that publicity is an ongoing process. Start publicity before, during, and after the first project even if you don't yet have experienced help. Use one-page press releases that include the basic who, what, when, where, and whys of the project. Send these out four weeks in advance of the project. Send a revised version two weeks before the event. Follow up the releases with phone calls to the most important media contacts to make sure they will run the pieces. Lists of media contacts are usually available through the United Way, public information offices at government agencies, or other volunteer organizations.

There are also many other ways to publicize first projects, including: speaking at meetings of other organizations; posters; public service announcements; word of mouth; articles in newsletters (your group's and others); bulletin boards at local outdoor stores, companies, and agencies; and interviews.

But group projects should not be the only focus of publicity. Begin a campaign of more general publicity as soon as possible. These pieces should promote the organization and its unique and crucial mission. Always remember to include a contact person in everything that goes out. Look to related events that might have tie-ins with your organization's overall mission such as Earth Day celebrations, community cleanups, or local land protection initiatives. Consider such things as interviews on radio and television talk shows, spots on evening magazine television shows, bumper stickers, billboards, your message on shopping bags, utility bills, T-shirts, and hats. Visibility and name recognition are key.

PRACTICAL POINTER

1. Try to recruit a talented publicity professional for the board or, better yet, as an officer. His/her professional contacts and skills, coupled with a serious commitment to the organization, can be a dynamic combination. Volunteers for Outdoor Washington, for instance, recruited a regional magazine publisher as their first president. This resulted in several articles and editorials supporting VOW and an at-cost VOW membership insert in 58,000 copies of the magazine.

■ ■ ■

Membership

Members are people who feel strongly enough about the organization's mission to join. Most organizations charge a fee or dues for this privilege, although some groups simply keep a mailing list of people who have expressed interest in what they do. For most grassroots organizations, it is best to set up a paying membership as soon as possible. Membership dues are an important source of predictable income for volunteer groups, especially ones that are just getting started. Paying dues also gives the member a vested interest in the health and performance of the organization as well as a structured way to make a modest annual donation.

Many grassroots conservation organizations initially oppose setting up a paying membership program. They reason that the time their members volunteer on projects is contribution enough and that many of the people they attract are already members of several other organizations that charge dues. Remember, if people believe in your mission, they will also believe that being asked to support this mission by paying membership dues is legitimate. Membership income can also be crucial to organizational survival. It pays for postage, for newsletters informing members of upcoming events and relevant issues, and for other incidental expenses that help to keep the organization going.

One way to set up a membership program is to establish membership categories with a sliding scale of dues. Dues for individual members might range from $10 to $25. The most expensive category would be for the "life" or "benefactor" member with rates that range from $200 to $500. The following example is the membership categories first established by Volunteers for Outdoor Washington:

$15 youth/senior

$25 adult (individual)

$30 family

$50 contributing (individual)

$100 supporting (individual/family)

$150 sustaining (individual/family)

$500 life (individual)

Recruiting paying members can be an exciting challenge for those interested in marketing and in seeing tangible, relatively quick results from their efforts. Try these and other techniques to attract new members:

1. Run at least two "recruiting projects/events" each year. These may resemble the organization's normal hands-on projects with the important difference that they are designed with recruiting new volunteers and members as the primary objective.

2. Have membership materials available at all projects and actively, but tastefully, try to sign up participants as paying members.

3. Mail a one- or two-page membership appeal letter and organization brochure to prospective members. Develop lists of prospects and beg, borrow, or buy mailing lists of people who may be interested in your cause.

4. Use phoneathons to contact and recruit prospects.

5. Sponsor contests and give prizes to members who sign up the most new members during a certain period.

Remember, signing up new members is only half the battle. Integrating new recruits into the program and getting them actively involved as well as retaining members year after year is crucial. Be creative in making new members feel welcomed and needed.

New members can participate immediately in projects that don't require special skills but give a sense of responsibility.

PRACTICAL POINTERS

1. Make each member's renewal date his/her annual anniversary of joining. This spreads out the membership income and the work of maintaining the membership records.

2. Send two progressively stronger renewal notices before canceling a member.

3. A personal computer with word processing capability and a simple data base management program facilitate membership record keeping and follow-up.

4. In addition to having project crew leaders get to know and recruit their crew members during the projects, consider making crew leaders responsible for telephoning each of their crew members within ten days of the project to:

   ▪ Thank them for participating.

   ▪ Invite the most capable participants to the next appropriate meeting.

   ▪ Invite them to the next project.

   ▪ Ask them to become members.

5. Specifically add "recruit five new volunteers and members each year" to every job description in the organization.

The key here is to operate on a *personal* level. Setting up a phone bank system ensures that new members get a personal invitation to their first project and to volunteer in other ways. Providing space or a checklist on the membership application for new members to indicate their personal interests is also good. Make sure that new members are promptly asked to volunteer in their area(s) of interest. New members nights, where new members enjoy a potluck dinner and a program about the organization, also serve to welcome and motivate new members. Many will appreciate this special effort that is made just for them.

Leadership Development

Strong, effective leadership is essential to a grassroots conservation organization's ability to accomplish its mission. Land managers, funders, and leaders of other organizations are much more receptive to working with a grassroots organization that has stable and reliable leadership. This gives them the assurance that the organization can meet its responsibilities over time. Before you try starting up a grassroots conservation organization, ask yourself if you and your cohorts have the following:

1. *Belief in the Cause.* Are you committed to seeing the work through?

2. *Ambition/Drive.* Are you self-starters?

3. *Courage.* Are you willing to try something different or new?

4. *Persistence.* Are you willing to keep on trying?

5. *Faith.* Do you have faith in yourselves, others, and the mission of the organization?

6. *Integrity.* Are you consistent and honest over time?

Volunteer leadership requires commitment, flexibility, people skills, and lots of hard work: AMC volunteer leader Carl Demrow with trail measuring wheel.

7. *Creativity.* Do you possess imagination and the ability to see things from a variety of perspectives?

8. *Sense of Justice.* Do you show fairness and respect for self and others?

9. *Flexibility.* Do you appear willing to learn and to change with external and internal circumstances?

10. *Decisiveness.* Do you have clear objectives and the willingness to act to achieve those objectives?

11. *Skill with People.* Can you work effectively with others, even those who don't agree with you?

Although it is unrealistic to expect each leader to demonstrate all of the traits listed above all of the time, the core leadership should possess most of them. This core leadership, as a group, will then be likely to behave in the following important ways:

- Demonstrates confidence in its ability to manage people and their work.

- Understands the task to be done and sets appropriate standards to complete tasks and to assure quality.

- Is approachable and supportive.

- Understands its role as a teambuilder.

- Is willing to be held accountable even if everyone is involved in the decision-making process.

- Uses problem-solving and decision-making skills that are appropriate for the tasks to be accomplished. Is comfortable with the responsibility for making final decisions.

- Understands the need for effective, open communication between leaders and team members and among team members themselves.

- Demonstrates a sense of humor, a willingness to laugh at him/herself, and an ability to separate personal interests from team responsibilities.

- Demonstrates the ability to delegate responsibilities to team members appropriately.

- Nurtures and develops the leadership potential of team members.

- Is able to convince other people of the importance of the organization's mission and to recruit new members.

- Works effectively with other organizations to accomplish the group's mission.

- Demonstrates flexible approaches to the solutions of problems depending upon the situation, the task, and the individuals involved.

PRACTICAL POINTERS

1. Remember that leadership needs change over time and may differ depending on the situation. Always evaluate the needs of the situation before recruiting a leader. Do not assume one leader (or small group of leaders) can be equally effective in all situations. The person who had the vision and energy to get the organization off the ground may not have the management skills to serve effectively as its first president.

2. Make sure each leader understands that he/she is responsible for recruiting, grooming, and training his/her replacement.

3. Find and use resources such as books, workshops, and consultants to develop leaders as a group and individually. Allocate resources each year for this purpose.

■ ■ ■

Motivation

Any organization will fail if its members are not motivated. Successful grassroots organizations have leaders and workers who are enthusiastic about and committed to accomplishing the goals of the group both in the short and long term. To foster motivation:

- Create an exciting, meaningful vision for the organization.

- Keep the activities of the group focused on realizing this vision and make these activities fun.

- Set short and long-term goals and objectives that are specific, demanding without being overwhelming, and agreed upon by members charged with accomplishing them.
- Create opportunities for members to successfully complete organizational tasks and praise this success.
- Recognize that every person is motivated by different things and act accordingly.

PRACTICAL POINTERS

1. Make sure the mission statement is relevant and inspiring. Keep it in everyone's mind.

2. Remember that volunteer needs change over time. In order for individuals to stay motivated, the needs of the person and the organization must coincide. Work on understanding and responding to the needs of volunteers.

3. Feedback is crucial to motivation. People want to know how they are doing and ways to do even better. Be generous with positive feedback. Don't assume that people know that they are doing a good job.

4. Review accomplishments and set new goals regularly.

5. Bring in new blood continuously.

∎∎∎

Team Building

Team development is critical to the success of a grassroots conservation organization for a number of reasons. First, no one person can do the work of the organization alone. Many tasks (particularly action-oriented projects) require the expertise, the energy, and the vision of a group of people working well together. Second, effective groups are synergistic. They tend to make better and more creative decisions than individuals working alone. Third, effective teams help build commitment. Team members feel loyal not only to the organization's mission but also to their group. They will continue to work on organizational projects because of their allegiance to and connectedness with their group. Fourth, working with others is more motivating for most of us. Being part of a group fills our needs for camaraderie and support. A team that works well together is more fun than working alone.

Because effective teams are so important to grassroots organizations, team development is the job of each individual leader and of the team members themselves. It requires commitment and on-going effort to develop a team with the following qualities:

A Sense of Purpose. Clear goals, shared and understood by all.

Open Communication. Direct and honest with no hidden agendas. Demonstrated listening skills, flexibility, and trust among members. All members are listened to.

Clarity and Flexibility of Roles. Knowledge of what each person brings to the group and what each is expected to do. If needs for new roles arise or if old roles must be modified, members respond positively to these needs.

Mutual Respect. Acceptance of each member for the value of what he/she brings to the team.

Ability to Make Good Decisions. Group works to achieve consensus. Differences of opinion are respected and viewed as a way to improve decisions. Members commit to decisions made.

PRACTICAL POINTERS

1. Have a board retreat shortly after new leaders are elected each year. Spend a full day or weekend helping the group get to know each other and work together. Consider having a skilled outside facilitator manage part of the session.

2. Have the board and committee heads work together during a project. Getting their hands dirty in the field is a great way to build group cohesiveness.

3. Make sure everyone has the opportunity to participate and to contribute. Draw out the more timid members of the team and help them become more productive.

Willingness to Evaluate. Progress toward goals is regularly reviewed. Appropriateness of roles, procedures, and focus regularly questioned. Changes made when appropriate.

Half the Work and Twice the Fun!

Building a successful grassroots organization takes energy, creativity, and commitment. However, the payoffs for your work are enormous. Working together in a group, volunteers can make a substantial impact on conservation issues. And as you can see from the examples in this book, organized groups of volunteers did far more than these same volunteers could ever do as individuals. When people work together, the whole effort is more than the sum of its parts.

Not only does working together let you accomplish more, but it is more fun. Working with others who share your values can, and should, be more enjoyable than working alone. In fact, with no exceptions, the most successful grassroots conservation organizations are the ones that make sure the participants are having a good time.

Why is having a good time so important? While successful grassroots organizations fulfill a very serious purpose, even the most useful fieldwork or crucial meeting can be pretty tedious or downright unpleasant. Without a spark of zaniness or a cold drink and laughs at the end of a workday, many of us would watch TV instead of heading out to the next project or committee meeting. But if we have fun as well as accomplishing something meaningful, we'll bring our friends to the next project with us and write about it in the company newsletter.

Fun starts at the top and permeates the entire organization. A "culture of fun" leads people to expect a good time when they participate in your activities. Having fun doesn't mean that we don't take our work seriously or feel that the group's mission is not important. It means that we realize that fun is the grease that keeps the machine running well. Fun really can make the job feel like half the work.

When thinking about how to create a culture of fun, remember to fit the fun to the folks. Different things are appropriate for different people and situations. A casual atmosphere and a few light comments might lighten an overly serious board meeting. A capture the flag game while armed with buckets of mud might be just the thing after a daylong project. Here are a few creative ideas for infusing fun into a group's activities:

- Parties after projects.
- Competition among crews.

A cookout at the end of a work day shows an important volunteer principle: make it fun!

- Crew songs and "uniforms" (T-shirts, caps—how about white laboratory coats for a quality control team?).

- Gag prizes at end of projects (The Day's Muddiest Volunteer, or crew member voted "Most Likely to Eat the Most Free Doughnuts").

- "Sign" your work (e.g. encourage crew members to sign their names on the underside of water bars, rock steps, etc.).

- Bury time capsules under trails/facilities.

- A crew "Olympics" (e.g., go for the gold in water bar trenching, the crowbar "javelin throw," "speed-cutting" thorn bushes, envelope stuffing, etc.).

- Nonwork outings (bird walks, urban hikes...).

- Ceremonies, awards.

- Social events.

- Caricature of crew leaders for the walls of the office.

- Scrapbooks and photographs.

PRACTICAL POINTERS

1. Take pictures of people having fun at projects and other events and use them liberally in newsletters and other publications. Collect fun quotes and anecdotes for the same purposes.

2. If a "Social Committee" sounds too stuffy, appoint a Fun Czar. Give him/her a generous budget and *no* guidelines.

■ ■ ■

Conservation work is extremely important. The needs are great and the opportunities are unlimited. But getting involved in conservation work does not have to be an overwhelming and somber crusade. Grassroots conservation organizations can take on crucial work that is important to them and accomplish it in enjoyable ways—ways that can attract people who would never consider becoming a "conservationist." With enough grassroots conservation organizations involving more and more "nonconservationists," we can meet the challenges close to home and then beyond. All we need is the spark that is willing to ignite the next hands-on project and then the next organization, then the one after that....

You are that spark! We hope this book has given you some ideas that will make it easier for you to get others involved and get another grassroots conservation organization established. It is a labor of love, but unlike many others, this one can be a tremendous amount of fun and can make a real difference in our world and in the world we will hand over to its next tenants—our children. You *will* make a difference!

Appendix A

Sample Timetable for a Volunteer Conservation Group

WHAT FOLLOWS is a sample two-year timetable for a grassroots conservation organization. It incorporates the plans set forth in Phases One and Two of this book. Each block represents one month, with activities and processes longer than one month in duration represented by shaded bars.

This chronology is just one example of how a group's work may proceed. Projects and activities will natrually vary from group to group. What is most important to note here is the relationship of activities to one another, and to the overall effort. Note, for example, at the beginning of the chronology that cultivating local support and searching for seed money precedes the group's first project. Note also (to give another example) that fund-raising and membership development are permanent aspects of a more structured, long-term group's work, supporting all other activities.

You may want to use this chronology as a "road map," but remember: your own experiene and local needs are the best guide to putting together your conservation work.

24-MONTH CHRONOLOGY

1 PHASE ONE	2	3
Assess need and feasibility		
Determine the availability of seed money		
	Cultivate local support	
	Form steering committee	

7	8	9
Recruit and integrate volunteers from projects		
Run second project		*Run third project*

13	14	15
bership development	*Fundraising, membership development*	
Draft bylaws	*First annual meeting*	*Incorporate and file for tax-exempt status*
Adopt membership policy	*Elect board of directors*	

19	20	21
Fundraising, membership development		
	Run sixth project	

4	5	6
	Recruit and integrate volunteers from projects	
	Run first project	
10	11 PHASE TWO	12
	Write mission and goals	*Fundraising, mem-*
Build projects into ongoing program	*Second year budget*	*Activate nominating committee*
16	17	18
	Fundraising, membership development	
Run fourth project		*Run fifth project*
22	23	24
	Fundraising, membership development	

Appendix B
Selected References

General

Coppock, D.; Henderson, Y.; Holderman, R.; and Seeger, J. *The Nonprofit Primer: A Guide Book For Land Trusts.* Oakland, CA: The State Coastal Conservancy. 1989.

Moore, R.L.; LaFarge, V.; and Martorelli, T. *Organizing Outdoor Volunteers.* Boston: Appalachian Mountain Club, 1987.

Obus, N.; Moore, R.; and Martorelli, T. "Partnerships For Public Lands: The Appalachian Mountain Club's National Volunteer Project." *Appalachia Journal* 46, No. 1 (1986): 48–58.

O'Connell, B. *America's Voluntary Spirit: A Book of Readings.* New York: The Foundation Center, 1983.

Scenic Hudson, Inc., and the National Park Service. *Building Greenways in The Hudson River Valley: A Guide for Action.* Boston: The National Park Service, 1989.

Board Development/Leadership

Conrad, William R. and Glenn, William R. *The Effective Voluntary Board of Directors.* Illinois: The Swallow Press Incorporated, 1976.

Goble, Frank. *Excellence in Leadership.* Caroline House Publishers, Inc., 1972.

O'Connell, Brian. *Effective Leadership in Voluntary Organizations.* New York: Walker and Company, 1976.

————. *The Board Member's Book.* The Foundation Center, 1985.

Stringer, G.E. *The Board Manual Workbook: For Effective Boardmanship and the Development of an Orientation Manual.* The National Volunteer Center, 1989.

Welty, Joel David. *Welty's Book of Procedures for Meetings, Boards, Committees, and Officers.* Caroline House Publishers, Inc., 1982.

Fund-Raising

Financial and Technical Assistance Guide For River, Trail and Conservation Projects. San Francisco: National Park Service.

Bergen, Helen. *Where the Money Is: A Fund Raiser's Guide to the Rich.* Alexandria, VA: Bioguide Press, 1985.

Brakely, George A., Jr. *Tested Ways to Successful Fund Raising.* New York: AMACOM.

Brody, Ralph, and Marcy Goodman. *Fund Raising Events, Strategies and Programs for Success.* New York: Human Sciences Press, Inc., 1988.

Crimmins, James C., and Mary Keil. *Enterprise in the Nonprofit Sector.* New York: Partners for Livable Places and the Rockefeller Brothers Fund, 1983.

Flanagan, Joan. *The Grass Roots Fund-raising Book.* Washington, DC: The Youth Project, 1982.

Foundation Center. COM SEARCH Printouts. San Francisco.

————. The Foundation Directory. San Francisco.

————. Foundation Fundamentals: A Guide to Grantseekers. San Francisco.

————. Foundation Grants Index. San Francisco.

Grantsmanship Center. *Grantsmanship Center News.* Los Angeles.

————. Exploring the Elusive World of Corporate Giving. Los Angeles.

————. Program Planning and Proposal Writing. Los Angeles.

————. Researching Foundations: How to Identify Those that May Support Your Organization. Los Angeles.

————. Special Events Fund-raising. Los Angeles.

Gurin, Maurice G. *What Volunteers Should Know for Successful Fund-raising.* New York: Stein and Day, 1981.

Kiritz, Norton J. *Program Planning and Proposal Writing.* Los Angeles: Grantsmanship Center, 1980.

Mitiguy, Nancy et al. *The Rich Get Richer and the Poor Write Proposals.* Arlington, VA: The National Center for Citizen Involvement.

Pendleton, Niel. *Fund Rai$ing, A Guide for Nonprofit Organizations.* Englewood Cliffs, NJ: Prentice-Hall, Inc., 1981.

River Wealth: River Guardians Across the Country Fund-raising Ideas. Portland, OR: River Network.

Smith, Craig W., and Eric W. Skjei. *Getting Grants.* New York: Harper and Row, 1980.

Legal Issues

Land Trust Alliance. *Starting a Land Trust.* Land Trust Alliance, Washington, DC, 1990.

Lane, Marc J. *Legal Handbook for Nonprofit Organizations.* New York: AMACOM, 1980.

Treuch, Paul E., and Norman A. Sugerman. *Tax Exempt Charitable Organizations.* Philadelphia: American Law Institute American Bar Association, Committee on Continuing Professional Education, 1979.

Management

Argyris, *Chris. Reasoning, Learning, and Action; Individual and Organization.* San Francisco: Jossey-Bass, 1982.

Bradford, David, and Allan Cohen. *Managing for Excellence.* New York: John Wiley and Sons, 1984.

Connors, Tracy D. *The Nonprofit Organization Handbook.* New York: McGraw Hill, 1980.

Connors, Tracy D., ed. *Planning for a Change: A Citizen's Guide to Creative Planning and Program Development.* Arlington, VA. The National Center for Citizen Involvement.

Dale, Duane, and Nancy Mitiguy. *Planning for a Change: A Citizens Guide to Creative Planning and Program Development.* Amherst, MA: University of Massachusetts, Citizen Involvement Training Project, 1978.

Flanagan, Joan. *The Successful Volunteer Organization.* Chicago: Contemporary Books, Inc., 1981.

Guth, Chester K., and Stantley S. Shaw. *How to Put on Dynamic Meetings.* Reston, VA: Reston Publishing Co., Inc., 1980.

Hardy, Brenda ed. *The Best of "Voluntary Action Leadership."* New York: Association Press.

———. *Managing for Impact in Nonprofit Organizations. Corporate Planning Techniques and Applications.* Erwin, TN: Essex Press, 1984.

Hersey, Paul, and Kenneth Blanchard. *Management of Organizational Behavior; Utilizing Human Resources.* Englewood Cliffs, NJ: Prentice-Hall, Inc., 1977.

Rutman, Leonard. *Planning Useful Evaluations, Evaluability Assessment.* Beverly Hills: Sage Publications, Inc., 1980.

Setterman, Fred, and Kary Schulman. *Beyond Profit: The Complete Guide to Managing the Nonprofit Organization.* New York: Harper and Row, 1985.

Weiss, Carol H. *Evaluation Research: Methods of Assessing Program Effectiveness.* Englewood Cliffs, NJ: Prentice-Hall, Inc. 1972.

Wilson, Marlene. *The Effective Management of Volunteer Programs.* Boulder, CO: Volunteer Management Associates, 1981.

Wolfe, Joan. *Making Things Happen: The Guide for Members of Volunteer Organizations.* Andover, MA: Brick House Publishing Co., 1981.

Marketing and Public Relations

Bortin, Virginia. *Publicity for Volunteers: A Handbook.* Arlington, VA: The National Center for Citizen Involvement.

Kotler, Philip. *Marketing for Nonprofit Organizations.* Englewood Cliffs, NJ: Prentice-Hall, Inc., 1982.

Maddalena, Lucille A. *A Communications Manual for Nonprofit Organizations.* New York: AMACOM, 1981.

Public Interest Public Relations: Promoting Issues and Ideas: A Guide to Public Relations for Nonprofit Organizations. The Foundation Center, New York: 1987.

Sperry and Hutchinson Co. Consumer Services. *Publicity Handbook: A Guide for Publicity Chairmen.* 1976. Available from the author at W. Seminary Drive, Fort Worth, TX 76133.

Recruiting

Haines, Mike. *Volunteers: How to Find Them: How to Keep Them!* Philadelphia: Volunteer Action Council.

Heidrich, Kathryn W. *Working With Volunteers in Employee Service and Recreation Programs.* Champaign, IL: Sagamore Publishing, 1990.

Stanton, Erwin S. *Successful Personnel Recruiting and Selection.* New York: AMACOM, 1977.

Technical Assistance

Gray, Sandra Trice. *An Independent Sector Resource Directory of Education and Training Opportunities and Other Services.* Washington, DC: Independent Sector, 1985.

Leonard, R.E.; Spencer, E.L.; and H.J. Plumley. *Backcountry Facilities: Design and Maintenance.* Boston: Appalachian Mountain Club, 1980.

Proudman, Robert D., and Reuben Rajala. *Trail Building and Maintenance, 2d ed.* Boston: Appalachian Mountain Club, 1981.

Volunteering

Ellis, Susan J., and Katherine H. Noyes. *No Excuses: The Team Approach to Volunteer Management.* Philadelphia: Energize, 1981.

Greer, Jerry. *The Management Side of a Forest Service Sponsored Volunteer Program.* Available from U.S. Forest Service, Fort Collins, CO.

Kimball, Emily Kittle. *How to Get the Most Out of Being a Volunteer: Skills for Leadership.* Phoenix, AZ: Jordan Press, 1980.

Working with U.S. Forest Service Volunteers. Washington, DC: Human Resources Programs Staff, U.S. Forest Service, 1982.

Appendix C

Sources of Useful Information and Resources

Environmental Grantmakers Association
1290 Avenue of the Americas, Suite 3450
New York, NY 10104
(212)373–4260

The Land Trust Alliance
900 Seventeenth Street, NW, Suite 410
Washington, DC 20006–2596
(202)785–1410

The National Volunteer Center
1111 N. 19th Street, Suite 500
Arlington, VA 22209
(703)276–0542

National Park Service, Rivers Trails & Conservation
Assistance Regional Offices:
Washington Office
P.O. Box 37127
Washington, D.C. 20013
(202)343–3775

Alaska Regional Office
2525 Gambell Street
Anchorage, AK 99503
(907)869–2650

Mid-Atlantic Regional Office
143 South Third Street
Philadelphia, PA 19106
(215)597–1581

Midwest Regional Office
1709 Jackson Street
Omaha, NE 68102
(402)864–3483

North Atlantic Regional Office
15 State Street
Boston, MA 02109
(617)223–5123

Pacific Northwest Regional Office
83 South King Street Suite 212
Seattle, WA 98104
(206)399–5366

Rocky Mountain Regional Office
P.O. Box 25287
Denver, CO 80225
(303)327–2855

Southeast Regional Office
75 Spring Street, SW
Atlanta, GA 30303
(404)841–5838

Southwest Regional Office
P.O. Box 728
1220 St. Francis Drive
Santa Fe, NM 87504
(505)476–1881

Western Regional Office
600 Harrison Street, Suite 600
San Francisco, CA 94107
(415)484–3975

Photo Credits

About the Authors

ROGER L. MOORE is Assistant Professor of Parks, Recreation, and Tourism Management at North Carolina State University in Raleigh, North Carolina. He was Director of the AMC's National Volunteer Project from 1985 to 1987, and served on trail crews and other AMC conservation programs from 1975 to 1987.

VICKI LAFARGE is Professor of Management at Bentley College in Waltham, Massachusetts. She was co-chair of the National Volunteer Project and AMC Assistant Education Director. She holds a Master's Degree of Forest Science and a Ph.D. in Organizational Behavior from Yale University.

CHARLES L. TRACY is a landscape architect with the Rivers, Trails, and Conservation Assistance Program of the National Park Service in Boston, Massachusetts. He has been involved with the Bay Circuit Alliance and other volunteer conservation projects in New England, and holds a Masters of Landscape Architecture from the University of Massachusetts.

About the AMC

The Appalachian Mountain Club is where recreation and conservation meet. Our 53,000 members have joined the AMC to pursue their interests in hiking, canoeing, skiing, walking, rock climbing, bicycling, camping, kayaking, and backpacking, and—at the same time—to help safeguard the environment in which these activities are possible.

We invite you to join the Appalachian Mountain Club and share the benefits of membership. Every member receives *Appalachia Bulletin*, the membership magazine that, ten times a year, brings you news about environmental issues and AMC projects, plus listings of outdoor activities, workshops, excursions, and volunteer opportunities. Members also enjoy discounts on AMC books, maps, educational workshops, and guided hikes, as well as reduced fees at all AMC huts and lodges in Massachusetts and New Hampshire. To join today, call 617-523-0636; or write to: AMC, 5 Joy Street, Boston, MA 02108.

Since it was founded in 1876, the Club has been at the forefront of the environmental protection movement. By cofounding several of New England's leading environmental organizations, and working in coalition with these and many more groups, the AMC has influenced legislation and public opinion.

Volunteers in each chapter lead hundreds of outdoor activities and excursions and offer introductory instruction in backcountry sports. The AMC Education Department offers members and the public a wide range of workshops, from introductory camping to the intensive Mountain Leadership School taught on the trails of the White Mountains.

The most recent efforts in the AMC conservation program include river protection, Northern Forest Lands policy, support for the American Heritage Trust, Sterling Forest (NY) preservation, and support for the Clean Air Act.

The AMC's research department focuses on the forces affecting the ecosystem, including ozone levels, acid rain and fog, climate change, rare flora and habitat protection, and air quality and visibility.

The AMC Volunteer Trails Program is active throughout the AMC's twelve chapters and maintains over 1,200 miles of trails, including 350 miles of the Appalachian Trail. Under the supervision of experienced leaders, hundreds of volunteers spend from one afternoon to two weeks working on trail projects.

The Club operates eight alpine huts in the White Mountains that provide shelter, bunks and blankets, and hearty meals for hikers. Pinkham Notch Visitor Center, at the foot of Mt. Washington, is base camp to the adventurous and the ideal location for individuals and families new to outdoor recreation. Comfortable bunkrooms, mountain hospitality, and home-cooked, family-style meals make Pinkham Notch Visitor Center a fun and affordable choice for lodging.

At the AMC headquarters in Boston, the bookstore and information center stock the entire line of AMC publications, as well as other trail and river guides, maps, reference materials, and the latest articles on conservation issues. Also available from the bookstore or by subscription is *Appalachia,* the country's oldest mountaineering and conservation journal.

NOTES

NOTES

NOTES

NOTES

Begin a new adventure.

Join the AMC.

AMC membership is a great way to start a life-long adventure in the outdoors—and your membership helps protect our open spaces and natural resources for the future.

Join the AMC Today!

THE ADVENTURE BEGINS HERE
YES! I want to join the Apppalachian Mountain Club!

Name

Address

City   *State*   *Zip*

Home Phone   *Work Phone*

MEMBERSHIP CATEGORIES

❏ ADULT $40

❏ FAMILY $65

METHOD OF PAYMENT

I enclose $_____   ❏ Check ❏ VISA ❏ MC

*Account Number*_____*Exp. Date* _____

Signature _____

Appalachian Mountain Club, 5 Joy Street, Boston, MA 02108
(617) 523-0636; fax (617) 523-0722